Being W

CW00450047

Are you studying or working in academia and in need of support? Perhaps you're finding your work, study or personal life challenging or overwhelming; are experiencing bullying, harassment or abuse; or find your progress is being blocked by unfair, exploitative or precarious systems? Or perhaps you want to support a friend or colleague who's struggling? Whether your problems are big or small, *Being Well in Academia* provides a wealth of practical and workable solutions to help you feel stronger, safer and more connected in what has become an increasingly competitive and stressful environment.

This volume uses a realistic, pragmatic and – above all – understanding approach to offer support to a diverse audience. Covering a range of issues, it includes advice on:

- Ways to increase your support network, so you're not alone.
- Reflections and actions that encourage you to evaluate your position.
- Guidance if you are in a stressful, precarious, dangerous or exploitative situation.
- Checklists and agreements to help you identify your specific needs and accommodations.
- Signposting to books, websites, networks and organisations that provide additional support.
- Ways to build your confidence and connections, particularly for Black, Indigenous or People of Colour;

LGBTQ+; disabled or chronically sick; or other marginalised groups.
- Reflections on your rights and the responsibilities academia should be meeting.
- Tips for being an active bystander and helping others in need of assistance.
- Ideas for resisting, challenging and coping with unfair or exploitative environments.
- Suggestions for bringing you happiness, inspiration, motivation, courage and hope.

This book is a must-read for anyone who wants to address the need to stay well in academia, and will be particularly useful to those in diverse or disadvantaged positions who currently lack institutional support or feel at risk from academia.

Petra Boynton is a social psychologist and Agony Aunt who teaches and researches in International Healthcare. She specialises in addressing the safety and wellbeing of students and staff in academic settings.

Insider Guides to Success in Academia

Series Editors:
Helen Kara,
Independent Researcher, UK and
Pat Thomson,
The University of Nottingham, UK

The *Insider Guides to Success in Academia* address topics too small for a full-length book on their own, but too big to cover in a single chapter or article. These topics have often been the stuff of discussions on social media, or of questions in our workshops. We designed this series to answer these questions and to provide practical support for doctoral and early career researchers. It is geared to concerns that many people experience. Readers will find these books to be companions who provide advice and help to make sense of everyday life in the contemporary university.

We have therefore:

(1) Invited scholars with deep and specific expertise to write. Our writers use their research and professional experience to provide well-grounded strategies to particular situations.

(2) Asked writers to collaborate. Most of the books are produced by writers who live in different countries, or work in different disciplines, or both. While it is difficult for any book to cover all the diverse contexts in which potential readers live and work, the different perspectives and contexts of writers goes some way to address this problem.

We understand that the use of the term 'academia' might be read as meaning the university, but we take a broader view. Pat does indeed work in a university, but spent a long time working outside of one. Helen is an independent researcher and sometimes works with universities. Both of us understand academic – or scholarly – work as now being conducted in a range of sites, from museums and the public sector to industry research and development laboratories. Academic work is also often undertaken by networks which bring together scholars in various locations. All of our writers understand that this is the case, and use the term 'academic' in this wider sense.

These books are pocket sized so that they can be carried around and visited again and again. Most of the books have a mix of examples, stories and exercises as well as explanation and advice. They are written in a collegial tone, and from a position of care as well as knowledge.

Together with our writers, we hope that each book in the series can make a positive contribution to the work and life of readers, so that you too can become insiders in scholarship.

Helen Kara, PhD FAcSS,
Independent researcher
https://helenkara.com
@DrHelenKara (Twitter/Insta)
Pat Thomson, PhD PSM FAcSS FRSA
Professor of Education, The University of Nottingham
https://patthomson.net
@ThomsonPat

Books in the Series:

Publishing from your Doctoral Research
Create and Use a Publication Strategy
Janet Salmons and Helen Kara

'Making it' as a Contract Researcher
A Pragmatic Look at Precarious Work
Nerida Spina, Jess Harris, Simon Bailey and Mhorag Goff

Being Well in Academia
Ways to Feel Stronger, Safer and More Connected
Petra Boynton

Being Well in Academia

Ways to Feel Stronger, Safer and More Connected

Petra Boynton

Routledge
Taylor & Francis Group

LONDON AND NEW YORK

First published 2021
by Routledge
2 Park Square, Milton Park, Abingdon, Oxon OX14 4RN

and by Routledge
52 Vanderbilt Avenue, New York, NY 10017

Routledge is an imprint of the Taylor & Francis Group, an informa business

© 2021 Petra Boynton

British Library Cataloguing-in-Publication Data
A catalogue record for this book is available from the British Library

Library of Congress Cataloging-in-Publication Data
A catalog record has been requested for this book

ISBN: 978-0-367-18669-2 (hbk)
ISBN: 978-0-367-18670-8 (pbk)
ISBN: 978-0-429-19751-2 (ebk)

Typeset in Helvetica
by Swales & Willis, Exeter, Devon, UK

I'll never be able to thank these women in person, but they have inspired me for decades. Hopefully this book goes a little way to honour their legacies.

Helen Boyle (1869–1957) A remarkable woman of Sussex who changed the way we provide mental health care for those most in need, especially poor women.

Josephine Baker (1906–1975) An incredibly brave performer, activist, resistance agent and mother who was never afraid to speak up, even when it cost her dearly.

Contents

Stay safe as you read: As this book covers a range of potentially sensitive and upsetting issues, I recommend using this contents page to identify what help you need and what to anticipate in the text.

Acknowledgements

To Adam and Aiden, who I can't say were particularly thrilled about me writing another book but stuck by me nevertheless, and for Will for making sure we're always okay. I love you all.

Thanks to Helen Kara and Pat Thomson for inviting me to write this book and bearing with me as I *almost* got it finished on time.

I've lost count of everyone who's given me insights and feedback through my advice columns, classes and consultancy; I've tried to do justice with your ideas here. There are also many people who've contacted me anonymously through research, particularly to talk about bullying and abuse, and I hope you got the help you needed.

To the kind people who initially reviewed this book and suggested new directions and ways to make it work; along with the beta readers who came up with even more ideas for improvement.

I've also had invaluable input and feedback from students and staff at schools, FE colleges and universities, both inside the UK and beyond. Thank you for highlighting everything I need to bring in and helping make sure nobody is left behind. In particular, Lindsay O'Dell and Sara Spencer at the Open University and Ceri Butler at Brighton and Sussex Medical School.

This book focuses heavily on your support network. Thanks to Leah, Jo, Rach, Mel, Lucia, Nicky, Sue, Hollie and Vicci who're always there for chats and kindness. And to Sheena, Chris, Celine and Bebe who look after me even if I'm not caring for myself.

For everyone using Target Medicine, my advice columns, safety and wellbeing workshops, and Listening Services, you make me feel humbled and very proud.

To Aayush, Lekdhen, Aashish, Jampa, Nidup, Rurami and Vela. You're all over the world now, but an inspiration every day.

I promised Liam I'd dedicate this book to him. So I have.

In loving memory of Marcia Worrell and David Hannaford, both of whom died just before this book was completed. I know their values will live on within these pages.

1 Getting started, being well

Hello there!

I'm using the term 'academia' to cover a wide range of possibilities. You might be based in a university – an undergraduate, postgraduate or postdoctoral student; studying full or part time, with funding or paying your own way. You may be a cleaner, security guard, administrator, manager or other support staff; or working as a counsellor, advisor, lecturer or professor. Your work may be full or part time, or sessional. Equally you could be based in the third sector, industry, health or social care, development; or self-employed as a consultant or tutor. You might be an Independent Researcher, Para-Academic or be working in an alternative academic #altac role. You may be at the start of your studies, an early career researcher or anticipating retirement. You might be a minority or marginalised scholar or staff member. You could be based in the place you grew up in or have since travelled far away. You might have moved several times and spent most of your working life speaking a second language, or you may be holding down several jobs to make ends meet. You might be worried about keeping your job, be on a zero hours contract or currently job seeking. Whoever you are and however you found yourself in academia, or in the pages of this book, you are welcome.

A note about content

I'm guessing you are reading this book because you or someone you care about needs help. This book addresses a range of complex and frequently sensitive and difficult issues. We all react in different ways and I don't want to presume what you might cope or struggle with, so I have not used trigger warnings for each potentially distressing topic. Instead, to help you feel in control while navigating this book, the contents (p. xi) and index (p. 255) show what is covered where, and there are clear subject headings and in-chapter descriptions of what's ahead so you can anticipate or avoid sections if necessary. Each chapter includes links to trustworthy external sources of support, and all chapters are separated into smaller sections to help you avoid feeling overwhelmed. If you are in crisis currently you may find it more comforting to work through the book backwards from Chapter 7 and/or use this book in consultation with any support services you're using.

Chapters and issues you may wish to approach with care

Racism, ableism, LGBTQ+ phobia and sexism are addressed throughout, with particular emphasis in Chapters 1, 3 and 5. Suicide is discussed at the end of Chapter 1, including a *safety plan* to help you address any suicidal thoughts and feelings. Chapter 1 also describes numerous issues in academia including precarity, stress, abuse, prejudice, overwork and exclusion; and Chapter 4 lists what you may need to help navigate academia, which is designed to support you yet might still feel overwhelming. Bullying, conflict, death, poverty, racism and violence are presented in alphabetical order in Chapter 5. Mental and physical health symptoms and coping strategies are discussed in Chapter 6, including references to drugs, alcohol, eating disorders and self-harm, and with information about venting included at the end of that chapter.

Run a diagnostic

Take some time before you begin this book, and before each new chapter or activity, to ensure you're feeling up to it, and also allow yourself space to decompress. Trust yourself and seek help now if you need it, or at any time while using the book. It's fine to stop or leave things if they're upsetting you.

Don't be discouraged

If you're new to academia or have never experienced problems within it you might find the descriptions presented here frightening or off-putting at times. Yes, bad things are happening, but that does not automatically mean they will happen to *you*. Please remember this if you are neurodiverse and/or anxious, and (like me) prone to fixating on negative events that have not yet happened. I work from a standpoint that it's best to be prepared,

Chapter 7

so if adverse events do happen you can try to cope while knowing where to go to get help if you need it. And I've deliberately included reassuring and uplifting ideas to ensure even if you can't change things, you can feel stronger.

Getting the best from *Being Well in Academia*

The aim of this book is to help you feel stronger, safer and more connected. Not everything suggested here is going to work for you. Try being open to new ideas while also being flexible about whether and how you use them. I'd encourage you to *'take it, break it and remake it'* (Boynton 2016, p. 18) – where you may accept any information that's right for you; adapt it if it's appealing but doesn't quite match your situation; or change it to better suit your needs. Look for links! The interlinking circle icons in the margins direct you to related information elsewhere in the book.

Throughout the book you'll be asked to focus on different areas of your life, identify where you may need support, where you can help yourself and where to find other places to assist you. To that end, your phone and/or a recording device, a computer/laptop and/or pens and pencils, plus a notebook, may be useful. If you're spending any significant time on the book, ensure you've refreshments available and take breaks to stretch and reflect.

Chapter 7

The following features are designed to help you take forward the ideas in this book:

– *Reflections and actions* – you'll find these in boxes scattered throughout the text.

- *Checklists and agreements* – these are designed to help you recognise your situation and follow up with additional training or assistance, or to prevent problems from worsening while giving others crucial information to keep you safe.
- *References within the text* – citing books or papers that provide evidence for problems and/or solutions within academia to improve your working environment and protect your rights.
- *Hashtags* – directing you to conversations, support networks, awareness and activism on social media.
- *'If you found this challenging'* – not all suggestions will work for you so you will frequently be asked to consider why that might be and consider alternative ideas.
- *Find out more* – recommended books, websites, podcasts, videos, charitable organisations and other sources of assistance.

Disclaimer

This book isn't a replacement for legal advice, organisational transformation, or medical or therapeutic care. Sources of help that can assist you further are linked throughout. All resources and links are correct at time of publication.

Before you go any further, take some time to affirm how you will care for yourself by using the following adaptable statement:

My wellbeing promise

I have the right to:

Chapter 2 • Tell someone if I feel I can't cope alone.

Chapter 3 • Reach out for help should I need it.

Chapter 2 • Treat myself as kindly as I would a good friend.

Chapters 2 and 6 • Be alert to warning signs of hunger, tiredness, stress and ill health, and act on them swiftly.

Chapter 7 • Give myself time and space to relax and recharge.

Chapters 4 and 5 • Take all the breaks and holidays I'm entitled to.

Chapters 3, 5 and 6 • Avoid, where possible, people/situations that are negative or harmful to me.

Chapters 5 and 6 • Permit myself to refuse to help others if I don't have the energy to assist, and/or if they occupy a privileged position where they can find things out without my input.

Chapters 2–7 • Accept compliments, care and kindness.

Chapters 3, 4 and 6 • Make informed decisions on what information to disclose when, and to whom.

Chapter 7 • Nurture and nourish myself.

Chapters 5 • Celebrate and enjoy all my achievements, big or small.

Chapters 2, 6 and 7 • Seek healthcare, claim benefits and accept all accommodations I'm entitled to.

Chapters 5 and 7 • Protect my time.

Chapters 4 and 5 • Maintain my boundaries and not feel responsible for other people's actions, thoughts or behaviours.

Chapter 2 onwards • Assist others when I can.

Now add your own promises …

_____

_____

_____

You can update this promise regularly to suit your situation. You may also use it in teaching, research or support groups to help other people feel empowered.

This chapter sets the tone for the rest of the book, noting some of the current opportunities and threats that lie within academia while inviting you to consider your situation and needs.

'Your fork goes in your left hand. When you go to university you'll need to know this.' That's my parents trying to get me to use cutlery. I'm about five and I don't like forks. But they've got ambitions for me and, as first-generation college students, they're acutely aware of the barriers to accessing education. Unsurprisingly, I grew up seeing academia as a mannered, exclusive, special place where wonderful things can be learned and opportunities offered – so long as you held your fork correctly.

When I've asked other people what's brought them to study or work in academia they've noted the following ideas. Circle or shade any that apply to you:

I came to …

fulfil my love of learning	improve my job prospects	discover things about myself
build on my existing skills	prove to myself or others I am smart	travel
feel less alone	broaden my horizons	give me something to do now the kids have left home/ during retirement
earn a wage	achieve something I always wished to do	stretch myself
accept challenges	see the world differently	improve my situation
try new skills	discover new things	make friends
help other people	share knowledge	have fun

Having reflected on why other people came into academia, how about you? Why are you here?

Write a love letter to academia

Building on the ideas given above, write or record a letter describing the things you believed about academia before you arrived; your hopes and dreams; what you expected from it; what academia has given you; and why you are grateful for those things.

Working or studying in academia can be exciting, demanding and stimulating. Learning new skills; living independently for the first time; managing your time and workload; studying for assessments; joining clubs or societies; and generating ideas. There is a lot going on and much of it is positive, even if it is challenging. If we're struggling it can be easy to discount these positives, which is why I've encouraged you to begin with writing your love letter. It is also important to remember that it is *normal* to find aspects of academic study or work difficult, and you may need to practice, take tuition, learn to reflect and correct your work before key skills are acquired. Academia has the potential to be a space for exploration and growth, where different levels of effort and input will be needed.

What's the problem, academia?

Academia is presented as something precious, mystical and exclusive. We can all get caught up in the magic

(Afonso 2018) and overlook how it is also a place of exploitation, inequalities, inaccessibility, precarity, prejudice and abuse (Ahmed 2012; English and Fenby-Hulse 2019; Sian 2019). The narrative of specialness traps us into overwork, uncertainty, unhappiness and anxiety. We blame ourselves for not trying hard enough, not being good enough, not having what it takes to make it. We hang on because we had a reason for being here, but perhaps now we've forgotten what that was, or we have become so jaded and cynical we no longer care. Possibly we're just stuck and have no idea whether or how to escape. Maybe academia isn't a special place but simply pays the bills. Confusingly, it might be many of these things at any one time.

Chapters 3 and 5

Chapter 6

Chapter 5

Stressors and problems with mental and physical well-being have always been part of academic life, particularly for those in low income and isolated countries (Newson and Polster 2010). However, more recently noted problems include:

- A marked increase in reports of deteriorating mental and physical ill-health among students and staff (Morrish 2019; Morrish and Priaulx 2020).
- Rapidly increasing numbers of students and staff seeking counseling or other therapies (UCU 2019).
- Reduced community mental health provision, austerity policies and disability sanctions (TUC 2016; McRuer 2018; Ryan 2019), contrasted by the World Health Organisation recognising 'burnout' as an occupational disorder.
- Fewer services offering study skills or other student support in or outside academia, leaving students struggling to cope – particularly minority and marginalised ones (Auerbach et al. 2018; Lipson et al. 2018).

- Competition over grades (Chang 2017), student work-load, increased fees and a culture of perfectionism (Koch 2018; Flynn et al. 2019; Kiziela et al. 2019).
- Minority students are still less likely to enter university (The Pell Institute 2016; Harrison 2017; Busby 2018a; D'Evelyn et al. 2018; NEON 2019); more likely to encounter discrimination over grading (NSC Research Centre 2017); and experience prejudice about sexuality, race, disability or gender from other staff and students (NUS 2014; Busby 2018b; Stonewall 2018; English and Fenby-Hulse 2019; Marsh 2019). They are also less likely to graduate (Hirsch and Lagnado 2010; Casselman 2014; NSC Research Centre 2019) or progress to senior levels (Rollock 2019).
- Job insecurity, availability and competition increase concerns for those leaving university with undergraduate degrees (Mok and Jiang 2018).
- Greater numbers of doctoral students are encouraged towards a decreasing range of university-based roles (Afonso 2018; Rasmussen and Andreasen 2018; Larson et al. 2014), with rising global unemployment levels for individuals with PhDs (FRED 2019). These individuals may lack additional training on skills that might gain them employment elsewhere (Passaretta et al. 2019), or lack an awareness of what talents they do have that might assist them with job seeking.

Chapter 8

- Issues around sexual harassment, violence, drugs and alcohol, alongside loneliness or other life issues, can make studying complex, with mental health problems appearing to be on the increase within staff and student populations (Hunt and Eisenberg 2010; Brown 2016; Flynn et al. 2019).

- International students may be poorly supported and experience high levels of loneliness while facing unaddressed racism (Chow 2013).
- Work-based pressure on tutors and supervisors alongside departmental cuts mean fewer people are available to confidently offer pastoral care (Newson and Polster 2010).

Meanwhile, over the past two decades, greater pressure has been placed on academics with the following consequences that create a culture of:

- Glorifying overwork (Newson and Polster 2010) and perfectionism.
- Increasing pressure to publish and bring in funding alongside short-term and precarious contracts (Smyth 2017; Bottrell and Manathunga 2019; Manathunga and Bottrell 2019).
- Rising student numbers and heavier workloads (Smyth 2017; Bottrell and Manathunga 2019) that place enormous pressure on academic staff, especially those from minorities (Brown and Leigh 2018; Estera and Shahjahan 2018).
- Teaching and leadership programmes that are neither designed to represent nor include diverse communities, yet may still claim to be making radical changes around inclusivity and decolonisation (Tuck and Yang 2012; Bhopal 2018, 2019; Brown and Leigh 2018; Prescod-Weinstein 2020).
- Neoliberal policies and practices, deliberately and strategically applied, have established an individualised, comparative, competitive atmosphere inflamed by university rankings (Fontinha et al. 2018) and student satisfaction surveys (Sanders-McDonagh and

Chapter 5,
pp. 121–122

Davis 2018); inflated Vice Chancellor/Provost salaries; and bloated management hierarchies.

- Moral panic around a lack of campus free speech (Grant et al. 2019), often fuelled by areas of the media and some politicians, and utilised by far-right organisations to mobilise attacks on minority staff and students.

At the same time many staff find their salaries do not cover their living costs; their personal lives are affected by their working conditions; their pensions are not always safe; and jobs are increasingly precarious. The atmosphere within academia may benefit those who are succeeding, but leaves others feeling frustrated, demoralised and lacking in confidence. While efforts have been made to understand and document difficulties faced by those in research/lecturing roles, others employed within academia, particularly in manual and administrative roles, are largely ignored (Newson and Polster 2019). It may be a struggle to work or study due to other negative factors surrounding you.

Chapters 3
and 5

While I was doing my PhD I noticed how my white, male, middle-aged colleagues had endless time to pursue their academic interests. When I asked one how he managed he solemnly replied 'I have a wife'. Academia is based on a white, middle class, heteronormative model (dubbed #thanksfortyping in recognition of women's hidden labour, see Savigny 2014; Perkins 2017), leaving everyone else disenfranchised. Conferences are a good place to spot this. They rarely cater for parents or carers (Calisi 2018); have social events centring around alcohol; are not always welcoming to early career researchers (ECRs); use presentation formats that favour confident verbal communicators, hosted in noisy, busy and inaccessible buildings with no interpreter services (Hodge 2014); and are places where sexual harassment, racism and LGBTQ+ phobia are frequently reported (Baker 2019; Dutt 2019; Smith 2019). Those who are one or more of the following groups may find themselves particularly disadvantaged and endangered by academia: disabled; Black, Indigenous and People of Colour (BIPOC); lesbian, gay, bi, trans or queer (LGBTQ+); people that have pre-existing mental or physical health problems; learning difficulties; academics from low income countries; mature students; parents and carers; and those who are neurodiverse. Where minority statuses intersect, the incremental pressures and abuses that occur in daily life may be especially difficult to navigate (Cho et al. 2013; MacKinnon 2013; Ahmed 2017).

Whole system changes across academia are needed to sort this mess (Gill 2009; Boyd 2019; Morrish 2019; Morrish and Priaulx 2020), but currently, despite industrial action and global campus protests, there seems little incentive from senior management to do so. Instead, organisations either implement quick fixes that fail to tackle the root causes of problems, gloss over or ignore issues entirely (Batty 2019; IRTC 2019; Morrish 2019), or run interventions, training, workshops or feel-good events that are often little more than box ticking designed to make academia look good while maintaining the status quo (Smyth 2017) – like a campus celebrating mental health month with a backdrop of student and staff support cuts, limited access to counselling services and relentless pressure to achieve. A day visit from therapy animals is lovely but will do little if you can't afford to eat or are being bullied every day. Or when 'wellbeing weeks' are the only time issues like mental health, disability and harassment are mentioned, with nothing done the remainder of the year to address accessibility, reduce racism or deal with abuse (see also Ahmed 2017; O'Brien and Guiney 2018; Morrish 2019; Morrish and Priaulx 2020).

As a consequence of the deliberate policies outlined above, bullying, harassment and abuse is a growing problem (Smyth 2017; Batty 2019); staff and student mental distress is increasing at an alarming rate (Brown 2016; O'Brien and Guiney 2018; Morrish 2019; Morrish and Priaulx 2020); and minorities still struggle to access academic spaces and face outright hostility and hindrance (Sian 2019). Unsurprisingly, many people just keep silent. Lots leave. Realistic opportunities for support, including counseling, occupational health care, wider health benefits, sickness pay, time off and retirement plans may be difficult to access due to financial cuts or the assumption that students and staff should be resilient and find ways to cope alone (Smyth 2017; Bottrell and Manathunga 2019; Manathunga and Bottrell 2019).

Chapters 4–6

In or out?

While sometimes it's easy to spot exploitation and inequality, other times it is not. I find it helpful when I'm reflecting on what's going on within academia to ask 'who is this bringing in? Who is it leaving out?' (see Boynton 2016, p. 118). It allows me to spot issues I may have missed, see different perspectives and acknowledge how other people may be struggling with issues that I take for granted or am not directly affected by.

Academic assumptions

We all have ideas about academia that may shape our attitudes, expectations, options, coping strategies, and the way we might assist others. Tick those of the following points that you believe about academia.

☐ Hard work will be recognised and rewarded.
☐ Inclusivity and diversity is encouraged.*
☐ Standards, regulations and complaints procedures will be transparent, easy to follow, readily available and applied equally to all, and an escalation of complaints will yield positive results.
☐ If you raise any concerns or make complaints these will be acted upon.
☐ Universities are dedicated to maintaining equality for all staff and students.*
☐ People will listen when you share any issues – positive or negative – and any ideas you have will be encouraged.
☐ Universities are keen to reform their curricula.*
☐ Nobody will cut you out of activities, appropriate your work or pass it off as their own.
☐ If you have any worries they will be taken seriously.
☐ If you are in crisis you can call security or other emergency services and they will attend promptly and offer help, not cause you further harm.
*Based on Sian (2019)

It would be lovely if all the above were true. They ought to be – just as all the ideas suggested in Chapter 4 (pp. 97–115) ought to be part of academic life. Unfortunately, however, for many in academia they are not. That is because academia brands itself as fair, impartial and quick to act in your favour if things go wrong (Smyth 2017; Bottrell and Manathunga 2019; Manathunga and Bottrell 2019; Morrish 2019, 2020). These may be assumptions that hold elsewhere in your life, particularly if you are from a privileged group where appeals to authority, complaints or sources of support are available, accessible and affordable (Sian 2019). Many readers will recognise, either from their experience outside academia or within it (or both), that life does not work this way. It can come as a shock when academia's mask of being decent, liberal, responsive, professional and impartial slips (Boynton 2016), or upsetting if you suspect academia isn't going to welcome you (or you have already had this confirmed) (Sian 2019).

There's no point lying. Things do go wrong in academia that are unfair, exploitative or even abusive, and you may have little recourse in such cases. However, just because academia is so flawed and biased towards minority and marginalised students and staff, it doesn't mean you should not try and use all of its systems and frameworks to make progress or raise concerns. Although you should always consider alternative routes to support yourself, including finding safer places to be if necessary.

Chapters 3 and 8

Avoiding the negativity trap

Reading the above it's a wonder anyone would want to be in academia at this point in time, and it's easy to get trapped into a mindset where *everything* seems terrible. I'm certainly guilty of it. However, despite the many drawbacks, staff and students stay because they are passionate about their subject, wish to make a difference or, more pragmatically, need to earn a wage. Previously in workshops I've asked people to help me make a 'good stuff list' as an antidote to the awfulness described above. Can you hold onto any of the following and make this list longer?

In academia ...

... you need to be	... you can look forward to
tenacious	pleasure
determined	excitement
bold	feeling energised
curious	opportunities
exacting	adventure
disciplined	friendship
persistent	welcoming uncertainty
thoughtful	anticipating complications
questioning	solving mistakes
realistic	overcoming disappointment
a fixer	being inspired
dedicated	helping others
optimistic	sharing
pragmatic	building

The list above is designed to remind you that many aspects of academia are supposed to make you think, give you pause and challenge your attitudes and beliefs, while stretching and strengthening your abilities. Focusing purely on the negative can be exhausting, distressing and worsen any current mental health issues. It can also make it difficult to celebrate successes, build confidence or draw strength to appreciate things around you (Ahmed 2017). This, in turn, can isolate you further and permit toxic messages of overwork, competition, individualisation and in-fighting to thrive (Bannon 2016). Resist.

Chapter 6

Chapter 7

The strengths and limitations of self-help

I don't think it's helpful to write you a self-help book without explaining a little about the genre. For many people opportunities to get advice are limited by finances, education, access to services, fear, shame and embarrassment. Self-help books, advice columns in print and online, or on TV and radio programmes, provide information people may struggle to get elsewhere, reassure them they are not alone, build confidence, alert them to danger and provide solutions within their immediate context. You can learn more about them here: https://nostartoguideme.com.

Self-help becomes self-harm when it's impractical, telling people what to do but not how to do it (Boynton and Callaghan 2006; Boynton 2007); encourages people to stop taking medication; culturally appropriates indigenous ideas; sidelines minority experiences or experts; centres white, straight, able-bodied, cis, monogamous, affluent people (Barker et al. 2018); and exploits the vulnerable (Boynton 2015; Hill 2015). This may be particularly tied with commercialised and celebrity driven messages (Boynton 2007), or 'consumer self-care', encouraging distractions to remove unpleasant feelings or mask distress – primarily with alcohol, food, shopping sprees and makeovers; or interventions that feel good but don't sustain long term (Mongrain and Anselmo-Matthews 2012; Bolier et al. 2013) while promoting 'recovery' without acknowledging this may not be possible or appropriate. Like academia, self-help can promote neoliberal ideas of self-modification, individualisation, resilience, relentless improvement and success (Boynton 2007; Barker et al. 2018), but not community organising, connecting or addressing root causes of discomfort or disadvantage (Yakushko 2018).

Chapter 3

How can you find helpful self-help? Look for advice that identifies problems, offers a variety of solutions to a diverse audience, accepts its limitations and encourages you to confront and challenge what's troubling you – not camouflage it.

A slice of advice

How do you like your advice served? Perhaps you want it boot-camp style, or reassuring and gentle? Cute or curt? Wordy or brief? Full of analogies to sport, the military, music, drama or nature? Feel-good quotes or barked instructions? We all like help in varying ways, and sometimes we might appreciate more than one message depending on our need. An idea that makes us cringe on one day may be just the tonic on another. I'm aware of our diverse requirements so have provided a range of options throughout this book. Remember that help seeking should be based on your need at any given time. You don't need to justify what brings comfort to you.

Why did I write this book?

For that you have to go back to around the time I was being instructed on forks. I always wanted to be a helper. I'd bring a first aid kit and flag on family trips – just in case anyone needed assistance. As a teenager that shifted into my daydreaming about becoming an Agony Aunt (advice columnist), reading problem pages surreptitiously during class and imagining what answers I would give. My teenage years weren't the happiest and I wasn't a stellar pupil, with an undiagnosed learning disability and told to leave education at sixteen, but I was also stubborn and so I got into university on a combination of spite and determination.

I did my first degree at Sussex University. It was the early 1990s and student politics and partying were as much, if not more enjoyable than my psychology degree, albeit within the spectre of Aids that took far too many of my friends too soon. I adored being at university but the experience came crashing down around me when I didn't get the degree I expected. My hopes were raised again when I got onto a PhD programme, but as a self-funding student juggling my studies alongside a variety of manual jobs, it was a challenge. Nevertheless, I passed my PhD upgrade, however a few months later I contracted Hepatitis A, became too sick to work or study, lost a baby, and my relationship ended. I had to leave the home I had bought, and my pets, incurring debts as I did so. I received funds from the college hardship scheme, but I hated having to ask. Due to misdiagnosis and inefficient care I was chronically unwell for most of my twenties, having to postpone my PhD several times, request numerous extensions, and frequently struggling to manage studying and lecturing alongside relentless pain, numerous surgeries and overwhelming exhaustion. It took me nearly a decade to get my doctorate and way longer to escape debt.

Around the time I was in a position to write up my thesis, things fell apart within my institution. My department split in two and I watched as people I'd known for years were bullied out of jobs they loved, forced into early retirement or otherwise ground down as things imploded. My PhD remained within the doctoral programme, but my teaching job disappeared overnight. I took the first job I could find and moved from Birmingham to London (I recently worked out due to a variety of reasons I moved over 14 times in as many years). I was excited to pick up a research role in the National Health Service, where I negotiated compressed hours of a four-day week, allowing me three days to write. It was a punishing schedule but I got my PhD. That felt like it made up for everything that had happened before, and almost, but not quite, helped me overlook how my personal life was a disaster and I was still broke. Ironically around this time I became an Agony Aunt, starting a career that's run across print, broadcast and online media tackling audience problems for places including *Men's Health*, BBC 5 Live, Channel 4 Television's *Sex Education Show*, and a variety of magazines and newspapers.

Unfortunately, in both the NHS job and the next one I found (again in a university), I encountered bullying – both of other colleagues and myself. It was a debilitating and frustrating experience, which led me to work with the *Times Higher* in 2006 to survey UK university staff and establish what was going on – abuse, harassment and prejudice was widespread (see Boynton 2016, pp. 182–192) and, at the time of writing, little seems to have changed (see *What's the problem, academia?* section above). Moving onto another lectureship brought me to a far friendlier department, but one where overwork was very much the norm. I pushed myself not only to publish and get funding but also to 'engage' and participate in numerous other career-advancing activities on an ever-growing list. Hitting academic targets was never enough, and the promise of promotion or recognition was always just out of reach. During this time I had my second miscarriage, although didn't tell anyone as I'd kept the pregnancy secret, concerned it would count against me career-wise.

Pregnant for a third time, this one went to term, although the birth was traumatic and I struggled for a long time afterwards with postnatal anxiety. Work, which had been enjoyable and secure for a while, now felt uncertain with many departmental changes and a similar structural fall out as I'd experienced during my PhD. Our unit shifted into a new division, many staff left and I remained to finish off our Research Excellence Framework (REF) submission. At the same time I had another miscarriage, then another pregnancy that again went to term, but I was very sick mentally and physically throughout. As a response my employer cut my hours rather than provide any accommodations, which I accepted through a mix of naivety, exhaustion, and the promise those hours would be reinstated after maternity leave. They never were. My second son's birth was easy, but the early months after his birth were very difficult with his feeding problems and my out of control anxiety and depression. I loved being a mum but, on returning to work, found presenteeism was in fashion, alongside workplace demands incompatible with childcare. About a year after returning from maternity leave I accepted redundancy after making a complaint of constructive dismissal.

It didn't put me off academia, where I now work independently as a consultant advising charities, government departments, universities and industry on topics ranging from the practicalities of doing research through to the safe-keeping of researchers and participants. All of these skills, the stories I've heard along the way, and the resources I've acquired are used within this book to support you.

Visualise your situation

You've read a little of my history and as you can see it's a mix of highs and lows. What would your story say?

At varying times in my life I've felt like I'd climbed a mountain, at others like I was on a rollercoaster or a racetrack. When lots of bad things happened in succession I felt like a magnet attracting awful stuff. How about you? Perhaps things feel like a series of hills and valleys, a deep and rapid river to cross? A calm pool or a forest clearing? Are problems sticking to you like burrs or blowing away on the breeze?

Being able to picture your situation allows you to reflect on what is going on; acknowledge what you've survived; recognise where luck, opportunity and privilege played a part; avoid blaming yourself; and note where assistance is needed. You can spot this by keeping a diary, or represent key life events on a graph, in a comic strip, on a map, or record yourself sharing challenging and affirming parts of your life.

Find out more

The following media outlets cover academia, providing news, advice and job adverts.

Inside Higher Ed www.insidehighered.com
The Chronicle of Higher Education www.chronicle.com
Times Higher Education
www.timeshighereducation.com
Guardian Higher Education
www.theguardian.com/education/higher-education
Independent Higher Education
www.independent.co.uk/topic/HigherEducation
Advance HE www.advance-he.ac.uk
University World News www.universityworldnews.com
Education International https://ei-ie.org
The Atlantic Education www.theatlantic.com/education
Eduwonk www.eduwonk.com
Chalkbeat www.chalkbeat.org

Wikipedia's list of student newspapers
https://en.wikipedia.org/wiki/List_of_student_
newspapers

I appreciate some readers will be struggling to keep themselves safe. The next few pages address suicide, including discussions around suicidal feelings and making a plan to avoid acting on them. There is also more information on mental health in Chapter 6 and ideas for calming and care in Chapter 7.

Make a #safetyplan

When you're distressed or in crisis it's easy to feel unwanted, afraid and alone. You may feel unable to ask for help or unsure where to go. You may not want to harm yourself or end your life, but equally you may be so unwell or unhappy you don't feel able to cope with the pain currently. Unfortunately the rates of suicide for staff and students in academia appear to be increasing worldwide (Boynton 2016; Universities UK and Papyrus 2018; Morrish 2019; Morrish and Priaulx 2020). A safety plan is a bespoke tool setting out what you need to help you address overwhelming suicidal thoughts and feelings. Knowing you are wanted, cared about and deserving of assistance are values that underpin these plans (Stanley and Brown 2012; Markham 2018). A safety plan can be used by anyone who has previously attempted and/or considered suicide, and their friends and colleagues, loved ones, family, trusted advocates and carers.

Safety plans are created by and for you – so you decide who needs to know about yours (ensure they are fully briefed on their role and if your plan requires them to take any action check they consent to do it, know what is required and are capable of it). Make a note of who's in your plan, including their contact details. You may also want to store this on your phone and let your workplace know who your emergency contacts are (many smartphones have an emergency SOS category – check in your settings to add contacts here).

Answer the questions presented in the following table to identify what will go in your safety plan.

Ask yourself …	*Note your answers in this column*
What are the warning signs that a crisis is coming (e.g. my mood, particular situations, how I'm behaving or feeling).	
If I have felt this way before, was there anything that either I or other people did that helped?	
Who do I want to stay safe for? (E.g. pets, parents, children, partner.)	
Why do I want to stay alive at this moment?	
Who can I seek help from? (List the contact details of key support individuals including friends, family, doctor.)	
I can calm/soothe myself by …	
I can be distracted by …	
What things might I use to harm myself and can these be removed from my surroundings?	

What personal strengths can I draw on? (E.g. my kindness, faith, good sense of humour.)	
The safe place(s) I can go to on/offline are …	
Other ways I can care for myself include …	
If I am unable to keep safe I will call or go to …	
If I stay safe today I will talk to my … (GP, therapist, Community Psychiatric Team, charity) … for further assistance.	

This plan was inspired by the resource created by Papyrus, which you can download or print here: https://papyrus-uk.org/wp-content/uploads/2018/09/Suicide-Safety-Plan-Leaflet.pdf.
To enhance your safety plan you can use the #StayAlive App, available from the App Store or Google Play.

If you need to speak to someone by phone or email the following organisations are here to support you (n.b., if you are feeling suicidal but want someone to help you reconsider look for organisations with 'suicide prevention' as their stated goals):

- International Association for Suicide Prevention – IASP (has a global map of the organisations in different countries that offer support and advice in diverse languages): www.iasp.info/resources/Crisis_Centres

- Staying Safe (UK) www.stayingsafe.net
- Connecting with People (UK) www.connectingwithpeople.org
- Suicide Prevention Resource Centre (UK) www.sprc.org
- Prevent Suicide (UK) www.prevent-suicide.org.uk
- Samaritans (UK) www.samaritans.org
- Befrienders Worldwide www.befrienders.org
- Louise Tebboth Foundation (for medical practitioners in the UK) www.louisetebboth.org.uk
- Lifeline (Australia) www.lifeline.org.au
- Wise Practices (Canada) https://wisepractices.ca
- RUOkay Stronger Together for Aboriginal and Torres Strait Islanders www.ruok.org.au/strongertogether
- Feather Carriers: leadership for life promotion. First Nations resource (Canada) www.feathercarriers.com
- National Suicide Prevention Lifeline (America, available in English and Spanish with resources for deaf and hard of hearing) https://suicidepreventionlifeline.org
- Living Works (Canada, US and Australia) www.livingworks.net
- National Suicide Prevention Alliance www.nspa.org.uk
- Zero Suicide Alliance (UK) www.zerosuicidealliance.com

You can also use a text-based service if that would suit your needs better:
- Give Us A Shout (UK) www.giveusashout.org
- Crisis Text Line (currently Canada and UK with plans to offer the service in Ireland, South Africa, Australia and Latin America) www.crisistextline.org

Or read these books:
Reasons to Stay Alive by Matt Haig (2015), Canongate.
You Are So Loved. Various Artists (2012), Chronicle Books.
Everything Is Going To Be Okay. Various Artists (2011), Chronicle Books.

If someone you care about is suicidal

You can share the safety plan with them and consult the organisations listed above for additional information, both for your colleague/friend/student and yourself. The resources for Suicide Safer Universities by Papyrus and Universities UK are also useful: https://papyrus-uk.org/suicide-safer-universities. It is important to seek help for yourself and maintain your own boundaries. You can offer assistance but you are not responsible for other people's actions, even if they try, or succeed, to end their life. If you are aware a student or colleague is suicidal they may ask you to keep things secret, but if you feel they are genuinely at risk you should take advice from the charities listed here and speak to others within your department or to student/staff support services if available. If a student or colleague dies by suicide you may feel that you should have done something more – more so if organisational factors led to the person's death (Boynton 2016; Morrish 2019; Morrish and Priaulx 2020). Collectively, you and colleagues may want to challenge the systems that caused you to lose someone you cared about. Support for you following the death by suicide of a friend or colleague can be found at:

Chapter 5, p. 142

Alliance of Hope (US) https://allianceofhope.org
Survivors of Bereavement By Suicide (UK)
https://uksobs.org
Support After Suicide Partnership (UK)
https://supportaftersuicide.org.uk

References

Afonso, A., 2018. How Academia Resembles a Drug Gang. *LSE Impact Blog*. https://blogs.lse.ac.uk/impactofsocialsciences/2013/12/11/how-academia-resembles-a-drug-gang

Ahmed, S., 2012. *On Being Included: Racism and Diversity in Institutional Life*. Durham, NC: Duke University Press.

Ahmed, S., 2017. *Living a Feminist Life*. Durham, NC: Duke University Press.

Auerbach, R.P., Mortier, P., Bruffaerts, R., Alonso, J., Benjet, C., Cuijpers, P., Demyttenaere, K., Ebert, D.D., Green, J.G., Hasking, P., Murray, E., Nock, M.K., Pinder-Amaker, S., Sampson, N.A., Stein, D.J., Vilagut, G., Zaslavsky, A.M., Kessler, R.C., 2018. WHO World Mental Health Surveys International College Student Project: Prevalence and Distribution Of Mental Disorders. *Journal of Abnormal Psychology* 127, 623–638.

Baker, K.J., 2019. Learned Societies Need Anti-harassment Policies. *Dean and Provost* 20, 6–7.

Barker, M., Gill, R., Harvey, L., 2018. *Mediated Intimacy: Sex Advice in Media Culture*. Cambridge: Polity.

Batty, D., 2019. UK Universities Condemned for Failure to Tackle Racism. *The Guardian*. https://www.theguardian.com/education/2019/jul/05/uk-universities-condemned-for-failure-to-tackle-racism.

Bhopal, K., 2018. *White Privilege: The Myth of a Post Racial Society*. Bristol: Policy Press.

Bhopal, K., 2019. For Whose Benefit? Black and Minority Ethnic Training Programmes in Higher Education Institutions in England, UK. *British Educational Research Journal*. https://doi.org/10.1002/berj.3589

Bolier, L., Haverman, M., Westerhof, G.J., Riper, H., Smit, F., Bohlmeijer, E., 2013. Positive Psychology Interventions: A Meta-analysis of Randomized Controlled Studies. *BMC Public Health* 13, 119.

Bottrell, D., Manathunga, C., 2019. *Resisting Neoliberalism in Higher Education: Seeing through the Cracks*. London: Palgrave Macmillan.

Boyd, R.W., 2019. The Case for Desegregation. *The Lancet* 393, 2484–2485.

Boynton, P., 2016. *The Research Companion: A Practical Guide for the Social Sciences, Health and Development*, 2nd ed. Abingdon: Routledge.

Boynton, P.M., 2007. Advice for Sex Advisors: A Guide for 'Agony Aunts', Relationship Therapists and Sex Educators Who Want to Work with the Media. *Sex Education* 7, 309–326.

Boynton, P.M., Callaghan, W., 2006. Understanding Media Coverage of Sex: A Practical Discussion Paper for Sexologists and Journalists. *Sexual and Relationship Therapy* 21, 333–346.

Boynton, P.M., 2015. Agony, Misery, Woe: A New Role For Media Advice Columns. *The Lancet Psychiaty* 2(3), 203–204. Plus supplementary online content (podcast) https://www.thelancet.com/pb/assets/raw/Lancet/stories/audio/lanpsy/2015/lanpsy_150225.mp3.

Brown, N., Leigh, J., 2018. Ableism in Academia: Where are the Disabled and Ill Academics? *Disability & Society* 33, 985–989.

Brown, P., 2016. *The Invisible Problem? Improving Students' Mental Health*. UK: HEPI.

Browne, N., Thompson, P., Leigh, J., 2018. Making Academia More Accesible. *Journal of Perspectives in Applied Academic Practice* 6, 82–90.

Busby, E., 2018a. Black People in UK 21 Times More Likely to Have University Applications Investigated, Figures Show. 23 April. *The Independent* https://www.independent.co.uk/news/education/education-news/uk-black-students-university-applications-investigation-more-likely-ucas-figures-nus-labour-a8314496.html.

Busby, E., 2018b. Racist Incidents at UK Universities Have Risen by More than 60 per Cent in Two Years, Figures Show. 11 June. *The Independent* https://www.independent.co.uk/news/education/education-news/racism-uk-university-students-campus-nus-incidents-a8390241.html.

Calisi, R.M., 2018. A Working Group of Mothers in Science. Opinion: How to Tackle the Childcare-conference Conundrum. *Proceedings of the National Academy Sciences of the United States of America* 115, 2845–2849.

Casselman, B., 2014. Race Gap Narrows in College Enrollment, But Not in Graduation. FiveThirtyEight. https://fivethirtyeight.com/features/race-gap-narrows-in-college-enrollment-but-not-in-graduation/.

Chang, A., 2017. *The Struggles of Identity, Education, and Agency in the Lives of Undocumented Students: The Burden of Hyperdocumentation*. Springer.

Cho, S., Crenshaw, K.W., McCall, L., 2013. Toward a Field of Intersectionality Studies: Theory, Applications, and Praxis. *Signs: Journal of Women in Culture and Society* 38, 785–810.

Chow, Y., 2013. *Race, Racism, and International Students in the United States*. NACADA Academic Advising Today. https://nacada.ksu.edu/Resources/Academic-Advising-Today/View-Articles/Race-Racism-and-International-Students-in-the-United-States.aspx.

Counting the Cost of Casualisation in Higher Education. 2019. Report. UCU. https://www.ucu.org.uk/media/10336/Counting-the-costs-of-casualisation-in-higher-education-Jun-19/pdf/ucu_casualisation_in_HE_survey_report_Jun19.pdf

D'Evelyn, S., Mason-Angelow, V., Merchant, W., Porter, S., Read, S., Trahar, S., 2018. Universities Need to Develop More Inclusive Practices to Attract and to Value Disabled Staff and Students. University of Bristol. https://www.bristol.ac.uk/media-library/sites/policybristol/Policy%20Report%2032%20-%20May%202018-%20Universities.pdf.

Dutt, K., 2019. *Race and Racism in the Geosciences*. Nature Geoscience.

English, R., Fenby-Hulse, K., 2019. Documenting Diversity: The Experiences of LGBTQ+ Doctoral Researchers in the UK. *International Journal of Doctoral Studies* 14, 403–430.

Estera, A., Shahjahan, R.A., 2018. Globalizing Whiteness? Visually Re/presenting Students in Global University Rankings Websites. *Discourse: Studies in the Cultural Politics of Education*, 40(6), 1–16.

Flynn, A.M., Li, Y., Sánchez, B., 2019. The Mental Health Status of Law Students: Implications for College Counselors. *Journal of College Counseling* 22, 2–12.

Fontinha, R., Van Laar, D., Easton, S., 2018. Quality of Working Life of Academics and Researchers in the UK: The Roles of Contract Type, Tenure and University Ranking. *Studies in Higher Education* 43, 786–806.

FRED. U.S. Bureau of Labor Statistics, 2019. Unemployment Rate - College Graduates - Doctoral Degree, 25 Years and Over.

Gill, R., 2009. *Breaking the Silence: The Hidden Injuries of Neo-liberal Academia. In: Secrecy and Silence in the Research Process: Feminist Reflections*. Routledge.

Grant, J., Hewlett, K., Nir, T., Duffy, B., 2019. *Freedom of Expression in UK Universities*. The Policy Institute, Kings College London.

Haig, M., 2015. *Reasons to Stay Alive*. Cannongate Books.

Harrison, N., 2017. *Moving on Up: Pathways of Care Leavers and Care-experienced Students into and through Higher Education*. National Network for the Education of Care Leavers.

Hill, D.W., 2015. Class, Trust and Confessional Media in Austerity Britain. *Media, Culture & Society* 37, 566–580.

Hirsch, A., Lagnado, A., 2010. Study Shows More Disabled Students are Dropping Out of University. *The Guardian*. https://www.theguardian.com/education/2010/may/25/diabled-student-drop-out-university-increase 25.05.10 25 April.

Hodge, N., 2014. Unruly Bodies at Conference. *Disability & Society* 29, 655–658.

Hunt, J., Eisenberg, D., 2010. Mental Health Problems and Help-Seeking Behavior among College Students. *Journal of Adolescent Health* 46, 3–10.

IRTC, 2019. The Final Report by the Institutional Reconciliation and Transformation Commission of the University of Cape Town. https://www.news.uct.ac.za/downloads/irtc/IRTC_Final_Report_2019.pdf.

Kiziela, A., Viliūnienė, R., Friborg, O., Navickas, A., 2019. Distress and Resilience Associated with Workload of Medical Students. *Journal of Mental Health* 28, 319–323.

Koch, A., 2018. *How Academic and Extracurricular Workload and Stress Impacts the Mental and Physical Health of College Students*. University of Dayton, Ohio, US.

Larson, R.C., Ghaffarzadegan, N., Xue, Y., 2014. Too Many PhD Graduates or Too Few Academic Job Openings: The Basic Reproductive Number R0 in Academia. *Systems Research and Behavioral Science* 31, 745–750.

Launder, M., 2019. *It Isn't Resilience that Nurses Lack. Nursing in Practice*. https://www.nursinginpractice.com/it-isnt-resilience-nurses-lack.

Lipson, S.K., Kern, A., Eisenberg, D., Breland-Noble, A.M., 2018. Mental Health Disparities among College Students of Color. *Journal of Adolescent Health* 63, 348–356.

MacKinnon, C.A., 2013. Intersectionality as Method: A Note. *Signs: Journal of Women in Culture and Society* 38, 1019–1030.

Manathunga, C., Bottrell, D., 2019. *Resisting Neoliberalism in Higher Education: Prising Open the Cracks*. London: Palgrave Critical University Studies, Palgrave Macmillan.

Markham, S., 2018. Online tool provides support for people with suicidal thoughts. *BMJ Opinion*. https://blogs.bmj.com/bmj/2018/12/21/sarah-markham-online-tool-provides-support-for-people-with-suicidal-thoughts/

Marsh, S., 2019. Hundreds of Students in UK Sanctioned over Racist or Offensive Online Posts. 6 May. *The Guardian*. https://www.theguardian.com/education/2019/may/06/hundreds-of-students-in-uk-sanctioned-over-racist-or-offensive-online-posts.

McRuer, R., 2018. *Crip Times: Disability, Globalization and Resistance*. NYU Press.

Mok, K.H., Jiang, J., 2018. Massification of Higher Education and Challenges for Graduate Employment and Social Mobility: East Asian Experiences and Sociological Reflections. *International Journal of Educational Development* 63, 44–51.

Mongrain, M., Anselmo-Matthews, T., 2012. Do Positive Psychology Exercises Work? A Replication of Seligman et al. *Journal of Clinical Psychology* 68(4), 382–389.

Morrish, L., 2019. *Pressure Vessels: The Epidemic of Poor Mental Health among Higher Education Staff*. HEPI.

Morrish, L., Priaulx, N., 2020. Pressure Vessels II: An update on mental health among higher education staff in the UK. HEPI Policy Note, April 2020.

National Student Clearinghouse Research Centre, 2017. Completing College – National by Race and Ethnicity – 2017. https://nscre-searchcenter.org/signaturereport12-supplement-2/.

National Student Clearinghouse Research Centre, 2019. *Signature Report*. Completing College: A State-Level View of Student Completion Rates—Fall 2012 Cohort. https://nscresearchcenter.org/signature-report-16-state-supplement-completing-college-a-state-level-view-of-student-completion-rates/.

National Union of Students, 2014. Education beyond the Straight and Narrow LGBT Students' Experience in Higher Education. https://www.nus.org.uk/Global/lgbt-research.pdf.

NEON: National Education Opportunities Network, Atherton, G., Mazhari, T., 2019. *Working Class Heroes – Understanding Access to Higher Education for White Students from Lower Socio-economic Backgrounds*. https://www.educationopportunities.co.uk/resource_items/working-class-heroes-understanding-access-to-higher-educa-tion-for-white-students-from-lower-socio-economic-backgrounds-2019/attachment/working-class-heroes-understanding-access-to-higher-education-for-white-students-from-lower-socio-economic-backgrounds-3/.

Newson, J., Polster, C., 2010. *Academic Callings: The University We Have Had, Now Have, and Could Have*. Canadian Scholars Press.

Newson, J., Polster, C., 2019. Restoring the Holistic Practice of Academic Work: A Strategic Response to Precarity. *Workplace: A Journal for Academic Labour* 32, 1–11.

O'Brien, T., Guiney, D., 2018. Staff Wellbeing in Higher Education: A Research Study for Education Support Partnership. https://www.educationsupport.org.uk/resources/research-reports/staff-wellbeing-higher-education.

Passaretta, G., Tivellato, P. and Triventi, M., 2019. Between Academia and Labour Market – The Occupational Outcomes of PhD Graduates in a Period of Academic Reforms and Economic Crisis. *Higher Education* 77, 541–559.

The Pell Institute, 2016. Indicators of Higher Education Equity in the United States. http://www.pellinstitute.org/downloads/publications-Indicators_of_Higher_Education_Equity_in_the_US_2016_Historical_Trend_Report.pdf.

Perkins, Y., 2017. "Thank you to my wife": unpaid work by women. *Stumbling Through The Past*. https://stumblingpast.com/2017/03/30/thanksfortyping/

Prescod-Weinstein, C., 2020. Making Black Women Scientists under White Empiricism: The Racialization of Epistemology in Physics. *Signs: Journal of Women in Culture and Society* 45, 421–447.

Rasmussen, A. and Andreasen, K.E., 2018. To and from a university career: Competencies and career strategies among PhD graduates in Denmark. *ECER*, Bolzano, Italy, 04/09/2018.

Rollock, N., 2019. *Staying Power the Career Experiences and Strategies of UK Black Female Professors*. University and College Union. https://www.ucu.org.uk/media/10075/Staying-Power/pdf/UCU_ Rollock_February_2019.pdf.

Ryan, F., 2019. *Crippled: Austerity and the Demonization of Disabled People*. London: Verso.

Sanders-McDonagh, E., Davis, C., 2018. Resisting Neoliberal Policies in UK Higher Education: Exploring the Impact of Critical Pedagogies on Non-traditional Students in a Post-1992 University. *Education, Citizenship and Social* 13, 217–228.

Savigny, H., 2014. Women, Know Your Limits: Cultural Sexism in Academia. *Gender and Education* 26, 794–809.

Sian, K., 2019. *Navigating Institutional Racism in British Universities*. London: Palgrave Macmillan.

Smith, D.K., 2019. A Personal Matter? *Matter* 1, 1439–1442.

Smyth, J., 2017. *The Toxic University: Zombie Leadership, Academic Rock Stars and Neoliberal Ideology*. London: Palgrave Critical University Studies, Palgrave Macmillan.

Stanley, B., Brown, G.K., 2012. Safety Planning Intervention: A Brief Intervention to Mitigate Suicide Risk. *Cognitive and Behavioral Practice* 19, 256–264.

Stonewall. 2018. LGBT In Britain: University Report. https://www.stonewall.org.uk/lgbt-britain-university-report.

TUC. 2016. *Equality and Mental Health in an Age of Austerity Report of TUC Seminar February 2016*. London. https://www.tuc.org.uk/research-analysis/reports/equality-and-mental-health-age-austerity-report.

Tuck, E., Yang, K., 2012. Decolonisation Is Not a Metaphor. *Decolonisation: Indigeneity, Education and Society* 1, 1–40.

Universities UK, Papyrus, 2018. Suicide Safer Universities. https://www.universitiesuk.ac.uk/policy-and-analysis/reports/Documents/2018/guidance-for-universities-on-preventing-student-suicides.pdf.

Yakushko, O., 2018. Don't Worry, Be Happy: Erasing Racism, Sexism, and Poverty in Positive Psychology. *Psychotherapy and Politics International* 16, e1433.

2 Creating your support network

Life isn't always straightforward, and you might have picked this book because you are struggling with work/study problems, personal issues, a health crisis or something else. Alternatively you may want ideas to help you care for someone you're concerned about.

Ripples

Picture a calm, deep pool. Now, imagine picking up a stone. It might be a small, rounded pebble or maybe a big jagged rock. Throw the stone – with a light flick of the wrist or a deliberate lob. What happens? The stone lands in the water, there's a splash and then … ripples.

Focus on the stone. All around it are ripples, moving outwards. Each of those ripples is a source of help. Depending on the size of the stone there will be greater or fewer ripples – your greater or lesser need for assistance. You decide what source of support to attach to each one. You could sketch this or annotate an image of ripples found online, or record yourself describing who or what is in your support network.

This chapter explains how you can create a support network. This is a powerful and important source of comfort and strength.

Six ways to centre yourself

Given what I said in the last chapter about the problems of individualisation you may be wondering why I'm focusing on you.

1 It's difficult to accept support if you feel unable, unwilling or afraid to ask for it. This isn't saying you must accept help that is neither wanted nor useful but an invitation for you to acknowledge that if you're struggling there may be a variety of things to try.

2 You're the one that needs to identify what's going on and where assistance is required. As poet Nikki Giovanni reflected in 1971 *'if you don't understand yourself you don't understand anybody else'* (see Baldwin and Giovanni 1973).

3 Realistically, the primary person available to help you is … you. Minority groups have known for generations to rely on themselves through sharing advice, community organising and neighbourhood support e.g. *Donde No Hay Doctor/Where There Is No Doctor* (Werner et al. 1970); see www.hesperianpress.com. If you are in an environment that is isolated or unsupportive, you'll need to find ways to protect yourself before seeking assistance elsewhere.

4 Ensuring you are taken care of is not an unreasonable act, nor is wanting to be treated with respect

and fairness. Audre Lorde's discussions on self-care have recently been given greater recognition, particularly with her statement *'Overextending myself is not stretching myself. I had to accept how difficult it is to monitor the difference … Crucial. Physically. Psychically.* **Caring for myself is not self-indulgence, it is self-preservation, and that is an act of political warfare***'* (1988, p. 130, emphasis mine).

Chapter 1

Here, self-awareness and support are not luxuries, optional extras, a performance or any of the problematic manifestations of self-help I told you about previously. Instead it's an act of rebellion and resistance. You value yourself, and so you care for yourself.

5   However without what ecologist @JacquelynGill calls #PragmaticOptimism, it will be exceptionally difficult to care about or for yourself. Focusing primarily on climate change, on Twitter Gill reminds us 'we don't have the luxury of inaction' (2019) using the hashtag #TeamMuskOx as an invitation to stand together with the strong protecting the weak. When life seems especially bleak and you are alone, uniting and being optimistic are major challenges. I've drawn strength from Harvey Milk's rousing 'Hope Speech', variations of which were delivered between 1977 and 1978: *'I know you can't live on hope alone; but without hope, life is not worth living. So you, and you and you: you got to give them hope'*, a line echoed posthumously by Raymond Williams: *'To be truly radical is to make hope possible, rather than despair convincing'* (Williams 1989, p. 118). These ideas give you permission to want better things for yourself, other people and the planet.

6 Optimistically, seeking support means being cared about, enabling others, gathering information and feeling empowered. Realistically there are aspects of academia and life outside it that may be difficult to change, exhausting to challenge and, on occasion, impossible to alter. Knowing we cannot always change the circumstances we are living in but may be able to address how we respond and cope within them are vital life skills (see Boal 1993; Bannon 2016).

Show and tell

You have talents and stories other people need to know about. Why do you love what you do? How did you get into the course/job you're in? Are you the first generation in your family to be studying/working in academia? Have you anything unusual or inspiring to share? You can let others know about you by using Ask Me Anything (AMA) on Reddit www.reddit.com; and sharing stories on Instagram www.instagram.com, TikTok www.tiktok.com, YouTube www.youtube.com or Twitter https://twitter.com. You can also volunteer on rocur (rotating curator) accounts on Twitter such as:

@500QueerSci	@Neurotweeps	@WeAreRLadies
@Astrotweeps	@IAmScicomm	@IamCitSci
@RealEngineers	@CMSvoices	@WetheHumanities
@WeRWorld	@MinoritySTEM	@wespeechies
@TWkLGBTQ	@WeAreDisabled	@WeStudentDocs
@SfPRocur	@AcademicChatter	@acreviewofbooks
@RealScientists	@IAmSciArt	@IndigenousX
@DatSciTweeps	@WePublicHealth	@SciForProgress

You can alert others to people you rate on Twitter with @RaulPacheco's #ScholarSunday: www.raulpacheco.org/2012/09/scholarsunday.

Or sign up to ventures like:

Unique Scientists https://uniquescientists.com
500 Women Scientists
https://500womenscientists.org
Made at University https://madeatuni.org.uk
Tiger in STEMM www.tigerinstemm.org

And share your skills with organisations including:

Skype A Scientist www.skypeascientist.com
Inspiring the Future www.inspiringthefuture.org
Better Make Room
www.bettermakeroom.org/get-involved

What do you like about yourself?

It's not a job interview so let's not start with your qualifications and skills. Tell me instead about as many different aspects of yourself that *you* appreciate. Like how you rescued your pet; your music, science fiction or sports fandom; how you've recovered after an accident; or the way your nose wrinkles when you smile. Why are you '*brilliant, gorgeous, talented, fabulous?*' (Williamson 1992, pp. 190–191). What have you done that has made a difference to others? What potential have you yet to fulfil? How far have you journeyed already – and under what circumstances?

Chapter 1

Make a list of as many positive personal character-istics as you can think of, e.g. friendly, kind, thought-ful, supportive, cheerful, attentive, generous etc. Fit them on one page, then circle all the ones that apply to you. Alternatively you could ask friends/family/loved ones to send a list of lovely words describing you.

If you found this challenging it might be because you have been struggling with confidence or esteem issues. Racism, ableism, LGBTQ+ phobia and poverty may have left you feeling you can't appreciate your body, your looks or your life. Past or current abuse or bullying may leave you feeling you have no right to feel good, or mean Chapters 3, 5 that you reject compliments and kindness. You may dis-count talents and skills because they don't earn you lots of money, come with a fancy title or win prizes. Rather than building you up this exercise may leave you feeling uncomfortable, exposed or anxious. It's fine to leave this for a while, returning to it if you feel stronger later, or to seek help (see later in this chapter) to address underlying issues through counseling, legal advice, life coaching or Chapter 6 career mentoring.

Be kind to yourself

Consider the following scenarios:
  Your best friend phones in distress after an acci-dent and you tell them they're overreacting or being unreasonable.

You hear a kindly neighbour calling out for you to help them but you ignore their cries.

You're babysitting a friend's child but you don't feed them for the day while they're in your care, nor change them when they're dirty.

You're teaching an anxious new learner – forcing them to do more than they're capable of, while constantly putting them down.

I doubt you would act in such needlessly cruel or neglectful ways to others, as in the examples above, but how often have you:

- Belittled yourself?
- Dismissed your thoughts, feelings, memories?
- Ignored signs of tiredness, hunger, discomfort or distress?
- Denied yourself nourishment?
- Didn't bother with personal hygiene?
- Pushed yourself to take on or do things beyond your skills and abilities?

Why? Have you been raised to be a people pleaser, putting other people's needs ahead of your own? You may not feel able to stand up for yourself. Or believe you are somehow undeserving. Perhaps past or current abuse has caused this, or studying/working in an environment where you are not valued or are put down and overlooked. If others are not treating you kindly it can be difficult to look after yourself, but this is all the more reason to put yourself first.

Chapters 4–7

Having begun with you, let's look at where else you may gain assistance.

Friends

Whether they are on or offline (or a mix of both), friends can fulfil all kinds of roles – sharing hobbies and interests, enjoying activities and events together, letting off steam or having people to sound off to. Different friendship groups might include people you've known since childhood; those you have met during your studies; or encountered through faith, activism, work or leisure. You might prefer a couple of really close friends, or a much bigger group of acquaintances.

If you are busy it's easy to let friendships slip, so put reminders in your diary to call people. Keep in touch via Skype, FaceTime, email, letter, WhatsApp, Instagram, Facebook or phone. It's also a good way to maintain your mental health and keep you safer within the workplace (as someone is checking that you are okay and you have someone you trust that you can tell if you are not) (see Boynton 2016, pp. 167–198). Setting aside time to care for yourself through hobbies, social clubs, talks or other events also lets you meet new people and allows friendships to blossom.

Chapter 7

If you found this challenging it may be you struggle to find the time for friendships; are shy or find social situations uncomfortable; or find your friendship opportunities are affected by your physical or mental health, neurodiversity, disability (including accessibility issues getting in the way of socialising) or income (it's hard to socialise on a budget). If you're studying or working in a country where you're not speaking your main language this can make navigating friendships more complicated, as can being much older or much younger than your peers, or being in a minority within your group. If you're frequently relocating for study and/or work, making or maintaining friendships and relationships can be challenging. In this case you may ask people in your place of work or study to help introduce you to others, or seek out mixers and introductions for new students/staff.

Alternatively, if you have lost friendships in the past, experienced prejudice, fallen out with friends or had people end friendships without telling you why (ghosting), you may feel hurt and afraid to try again. Fear of rejection can also make us hyper-vigilant, prone to pre-emptively ending friendships or may make us become overwhelmingly clingy. If friendships are a source of drama, counseling can focus on navigating friendships to reduce hurt, deal with rejection, act assertively and find people who you've got more in common with.

Your social network

If you're looking for places to meet people here are a range of options people have recommended:

- What's-on guides. Tourism websites. Posters/ bulletin boards.
- Campus/workplace events, clubs and societies. Libraries, museums, theatres, clubs.
- Professional societies/organisation talks/activities. Email lists.
- Introduction/induction events for new students/ staff. Social media groups.
- On or offline study groups and courses. Places of worship.

- Public engagement, networking and conferences. Activism and awareness raising.
- Online events (use hashtags to find online chats). Volunteering and fundraising.
- Hobbies and interests. Sport and exercise classes or clubs.
- Get-togethers you organise. Befriending and community organising.

Find out more

Mental Health Foundation's guide to friendship www.mental health.org.uk/a-to-z/f/friendship-and-mental-health

An Aspie's Guide to Making and Keeping Friends: Been There. Done That. Try This! Tony Attwood, Craig R. Evans and Anita Lesko (eds) (2014), Jessica Kingsley Publishers.

Making Friends at Work: Learning to Make Positive Choices in Social Situations for People with Autism. Saffron Gallup (2017), Jessica Kingsley Publishers.

College Info Geek's guide to making friends in college https://collegeinfogeek.com/make-friends-college

If you're feeling lonely or isolated you can find out more from:

Marmalade Trust https://marmaladetrust.org

Campaign to End Loneliness www.campaigntoendloneliness.org

Family

All families are different. Some are very close, physically and geographically. Others keep a strong bond no matter the distance. Still more share a connection without being especially demonstrative. For some, families are a source of tension or abuse. It may be safer not to be around our 'biological family', choosing instead what the author Armistead Maupin www.armisteadmaupin.com describes, in his Tales of the City series, as a 'logical family' of people *we* pick as our kin.

Your family may be a source of support – sharing household chores and childcare with you, cheerleading successes or assisting financially. You may welcome this and find it hugely rewarding, particularly if you're from a collectivist culture. Alternatively you could feel pressured by obligations (for example your role as a breadwinner or carer, or because so much is expected of you) or frustrated if your family doesn't appear to understand your area of study/job or are dismissive about academia. If you live with your family while working or studying it can be tense – especially if your accommodation gives you little privacy or peace. Anyone in your family can become unwell, struggle with life issues and need additional support from you, including financial obligations. You may also suffer if you are separated from your family – perhaps living in a different country or time zone and/or having to relocate frequently. Regular contact via Skype, email, phone or letter can reduce loneliness. This may be especially necessary if you are unable to travel home often (or at all if you are separated due to finances, visas, sickness or conflict).

Chapter 4
Chapter 5
Chapter 8

Some academic spaces are supportive of family lives, allowing time for attending meetings and appointments, having parent-/carer-friendly working practices or letting you reschedule work and holidays. For long-term conditions/situations you may need to negotiate your contract/hours worked or even change jobs. This may feel frustrating and upsetting so make use of any charities and organisations offering help. If you're a funded student, remember to speak to your supervisor if your family is expecting you to use that money to support them, as this may impact on your financial and visa situation.

Chapter 6

Find out more

Family Lives www.familylives.org.uk
Stand Alone www.standalone.org.uk
Susan Forward's books explain family difficulties and offer solutions on coping with toxic relationships: www.susanforward.com/author.htm

Relationships

Your relationships may be a source of pleasure, inspiration, connection and joy. Being able to share your time, feelings and worries with someone you care about can be especially reassuring. However, relationships can be put under pressure by distance, separation, overwork or other issues. Being able to meet, date and focus on partners, or sustain long-term relationships, can be challenging if you are busy, stressed or distracted.

Chapters 5 and 6

For those not in relationships, finding someone while attending to the demands of work/study can feel scary, upsetting and frustrating, particularly if being disabled, neurodiverse, LGBTQ+, from a racial minority or on a low income affects your ability to access social spaces or feel safe within them. Using the social networking ideas listed previously can help, as can trying online dating, apps, introduction agencies, speed dating, social mixers, match making and introductions from friends or family.

Relationship difficulties can arise at any time, but the specific stressors and work/study conditions of academia can make it more difficult to meet people, sustain relationships (particularly over distance) and manage partnerships (particularly if you have other carer responsibilities). It's not unusual for relationships to be adversely affected when work is stressful, or during periods of unemployment or career success. This may be because the time needed to invest in your relationship is centred elsewhere or your new job/qualification has changed your dynamic, which your partner may feel threatened by. Setting aside time to talk about your work/studies with partners while using other support systems so they aren't overloaded can help. As may sharing diaries to anticipate when busy periods are likely, offering support and scheduling work/study-free times when you can enjoy being together alongside other assistance with childcare, housework etc.

Chapter 5

If your relationship breaks down you can request compassionate leave and let people know if you're likely to be upset or distracted. Relationship counseling for you and your partner can help if you want to improve your relationship, reconcile or split as amicably as possible. Identifying your rights over finances, property and access visits if you have any children or pets is essential.

Chapter 4

Chapters 5–6

Find out more

Esther Perel's dating and relationship advice
https://estherperel.com

Troubleshooting Relationships on the Autism Spectrum: A User's Guide to Resolving Relationship Problems. Ashley Stanford (2013), Jessica Kingsley Publishers.

Flirtology https://flirtology.com

Outsiders (disabled dating and relationship advice) www.outsiders.org.uk

Stars in the Sky (match making agency for people with disabilities and learning difficulties) www.starsinthesky.co.uk

Decoding Dating: A Guide to the Unwritten Social Rules of Dating for Men with Asperger Syndrome (Autism Spectrum Disorder). John Miller (2014), Jessica Kingsley Publishers.

The Aspie Girl's Guide to Being Safe with Men: The Unwritten Safety Rules No-one is Telling You. Debi Brown (2012), Jessica Kingsley Publishers.

The Autism Spectrum Guide to Sexuality and Relationships: Understand Yourself and Make Choices that are Right for You. Emma Goodall (2016), Jessica Kingsley Publishers.

Love, Partnership, or Singleton on the Autism Spectrum. Luke Beardon and Dean Worton (eds) (2017), Jessica Kingsley Publishers.

Sex and relationship advice is also available from:
Meg-John and Justin https://megjohnandjustin.com
Scarleteen www.scarleteen.com

Pets

Whether it's the departmental dog, the campus cat or your pets at home, animals can be a huge source of comfort and companionship. Depending on your circumstances it may not be possible to keep a pet, but you may be able to help look after a friend or colleague's animal (some people take on pet sitting jobs to do this with the added bonus they might get a break or have some space to study). Alternatively, you may get a pet or use a specially trained therapy, support, service/assistance animal. You can also connect with others on social media sharing pet photos or hashtags like #AcademicsWithCats (or any animal you prefer, cats are best, obviously).

If you found this challenging you may have had to leave a pet behind due to relocation or a relationship break down. Or your pet may have died. Animals can play a huge part in our lives so using other parts of your support network to help if you've lost your pet or are worried about them can be reassuring. Not everyone feels safe to tell colleagues about pet bereavement, but if it's impacting on your work or study it may be beneficial to do so.

Blue Cross Pet Bereavement and Pet Loss: www.bluecross.org.uk/pet-bereavement-and-pet-loss

The Cinnamon Trust helps older and terminally ill people who are concerned about their pets: https://cinnamon.org.uk

Refuge has advice for those leaving abusive relationships that are worried about their animals: www.refuge.org.uk/get-help-now/what-about-pets

Colleagues/peers

Finding allies you can chat to, learn from or share work with can be vital for your emotional wellbeing and career progression. Societies and professional organisations, or workplace study groups, are an excellent way to connect. If you're struggling to find these networks, you could try setting up your own group.

Social media

Hashtags are a fantastic way to find folk. Instagram, Twitter and Facebook in particular are used by academics to share ideas, ask for help, get advice and foster opportunities. You don't have to join in a chat, you can use hashtags to locate others and read what they're saying. Or use hashtags yourself in conversations or to broadcast the fact that you need assistance. You can find plenty of them throughout this book, but particularly in Chapter 5.

If you found this challenging you may crave connection, but distance, disability or prejudice may keep you isolated. In this case being able to stay in touch remotely with those you do care about can be a lifeline. You can time contact to when energy and connectivity allows. For some of us, no matter how well connected we are, we can still struggle if our mental health is poor. If thinking about friendships or building networks has made you feel inadequate or anxious, and/or you're struggling with mental health issues, you might use it as a prompt to see your doctor or speak to a counsellor if one is available (see *Therapy* below).

Chapter 6

Other places that can help you within academia

Supervisors – these may include your line manager at work who should be responsible for your mentoring, career progression, ensuring you are correctly trained and supported, and who may issue warnings and disciplinary proceedings. For PhD students you will have one or more

Chapter 4

supervisors who are qualified in your area of study and who should offer regular meetings, either in person or via email, Skype, letter or phone, to discuss progress; guide your work; respond to your questions in a timely fashion; advise if things are going wrong; check proposals; ensure regulations are adhered to; read drafts of your work; help you apply for additional funding (if necessary); encourage and mentor you to disseminate your work; assist you with reasonable adjustments; and listen if you are experiencing other difficulties that might affect your progress. Your university website or handbook will have regulations setting out supervisor/supervisee arrangements, and you may need to formally complete a log book or assessment portfolio to indicate where supervision has taken place and what has been agreed.

Find out more

Helen Kara has a series of books covering all stages of the PhD process, available at
https://helenkara.com/writing/know-more-publishing
   How To get a PhD: A Handbook for Students and their Supervisors. Estelle Phillips and Derek S. Pugh (2015), Open University Press.
   A Handbook for Doctoral Supervisors. Stan Taylor, Margaret Kiley and Robin Humphrey (2017), Routledge.
   Support and information for students in secure environments from the Open University:
www.open.ac.uk/secure-environments/students-prison
   Staff/student counselling services – although increasingly these are being cut, some academic spaces have time-limited, free counseling support.

Student Support and Guidance Tutors (SSGT) – may also be known as Guidance Counsellors or Support Tutors and may either work within departments/schools or within specific units. They will host specific sessions to discuss academic and personal worries, accommodation problems, study skills, mental health or financial hardship. In some organisations they are open to students only, while in others staff may also use these services.

Residential Tutors or Residential Advisors – similar to SSGTs, these are students that live in university-owned residences and offer information on campus life while being alert to any students that might be in crisis who they can refer to other sources of help.

Nightline – a UK voluntary service run by students for students offering overnight telephone, email and text support: www.nightline.ac.uk. In other countries student groups and mental health charities offer similar services. Check your college website for more information.

Mentors – some institutions match new/junior/minority staff or students with more experienced colleagues for encouragement and practical advice.

Training and support is usually provided for supervisors, mentors, SSGTs, advisors and Nightline volunteers to enable them to offer pastoral care and other advice. If you are interested in these roles you can apply for positions and training or request it is provided by your institution. Many organisations have supervisor/tutor guides available on their websites that you can use if you are trying to learn more about what help to ask for or what care you might offer. Remember if you are offering any of these support services they need to be accessible to all staff/students and be well advertised.

Chapter 4

Human Resources (also known as HR, People Operations, People Resource Manager etc) – they exist

Chapter 4

Chapters 3–5

to protect the organisation you are studying with/working for. Despite this, they still have a duty of care towards your rights and wellbeing. You can find out about training, career development and workplace support from HR, alongside obtaining information on rules and regulations, raising complaints and grievance procedures.

Chaplaincy – if you are based in a university, prison or hospital there will be multi-faith (including humanist) Chaplains available for support, introduction to congregations and social events. Many offer hardship funds and access to Foodbanks and other services available, regardless of faith (see also www.nacuc.net).

Student Union (SU) – undergraduate and postgraduate students can get information about all aspects of college life, from navigating a new campus to entertainments and activities, plus advice on job seeking and study skills. If there are problems with housing, work or tutors/supervisors the SU can advise. You may want to become involved with the union both to support others and socialise, and can find out more from your college website or during induction/welcome weeks. Some examples include:

National Union of Students, UK
www.nus.org.uk
Canadian Alliance of Student Association
www.casa-acae.com
National Union of Students, Australia
http://nus.asn.au
International Union of Students
https://en.wikipedia.org/wiki/International_Union_of_Students#Members
Council of International Students Australia
https://cisa.edu.au
Int'l Student Organisation in the USA
www.intlstudent.org

Links to other student Unions can be found here:
https://en.wikipedia.org/wiki/Students%27_union
   Teaching unions – these exist to help anyone in academic roles, full or part time (including precarious workers), to safeguard dignity and rights at work. Union Representatives can also listen to your workplace problems, identify sources of information and accompany you to your workplace. They may also be able to signpost you to legal advice. Collectively, unions push for fairer treatment of all staff and students through organising meetings and industrial action.

Chapters 3–5

Universities and Colleges Union (UCU) UK
www.ucu.org.uk
American Association of University Professors
https://www.aaup.org
National Education Union (UK)
https://neu.org.uk
List of Education Trade Unions
https://en.wikipedia.org/wiki/List_of_education_trade_unions
International College and University Associations and Consortia
https://en.wikipedia.org/wiki/Category:International_college_and_university_associations_and_consortia
   Other unions – staff working as cleaners, managers, administrators, porters, security guards and caterers, amongst other roles, can also use unions to ensure fairness in working hours, training, equipment provision, pay and conditions. This may be particularly important for marginalised staff and those on precarious and zero hours contracts.
Association of Chief Security Officers (UK)
www.aucso.org
Association of University Administrators (UK)
https://aua.ac.uk

Unison (UK) www.unison.org.uk
GMB (UK) www.gmb.org.uk
A list linking to global unions covering a variety of professions can be found here:
https://en.wikipedia.org/wiki/List_of_trade_unions

Professional societies and organisations

These might be online special interest groups, subject-focused groups or peer-support networks. While some organisations charge fees, you can ask about student or low-income registration options. Some are excellent in regards to providing professional and personal guidance and opportunities for career development, employment and other networking events. Research online ones who are going to meet your varied needs and ask current members for honest feedback over whether membership is worthwhile. If organisations host any introductory events at conferences, or standalone talks, these may give you a sense of whether you'll be welcome and well supported.

Academic social networking sites (ASNS)

These are repositories where you can save your work, update on current or past projects, connect with others working in similar areas or request copies of research. Such sites include:
Zotero www.zotero.org
ResearchGate www.researchgate.net
Mendeley www.mendeley.com
Academia.Edu www.academia.edu

Orcid https://orcid.org
Google Scholar https://orcid.org
LinkedIn https://uk.linkedin.com
Our Research https://our-research.org

Charities

You may find charities that specifically support academics useful, while at other times you may make use of charitable support during your studies or work. Charities can also support you with money to fund books, attend conferences, travel or gain grants for further study.
Council for Refugee Academics www.cara.ngo
Education Support Partnership
www.educationsupportpartnership.org.uk
The Research Companion's useful resources
http://theresearchcompanion.com/resources
Author Aid www.authoraid.info/en

Underepresented minorites #URM

It may be particularly challenging to navigate academia if you fall within one or more of the following groups:

- #Disabled; #BIPOC (#Black, #Indigenous or a Person of Colour); #LGBTQ+ (#Lesbian, #Gay, #Bisexual, #Transgender, #Queer, #Nonbinary) individuals.
- Are in a secure environment (prisons and special hospitals).

- Are experiencing financial hardship, are old or are a woman.
- Are unemployed, have an insecure job or are on a precarious contract.

Chapter 1, pp. 8–14

Since minorities face discrimination within academia and outside it, having places to get specific support is helpful, as is having spaces where you can speak frankly among others that will understand your situation. If you are within a university, joining societies (e.g. LGBTQ+ in STEM or Black Students Society) is a good place to begin, while searching for minorities linked to your subject discipline or status (e.g. Indigenous Historians or Disabled Postdocs) will reveal other networks. See Chapter 5 for hashtags or try organisations others have recommended, such as:

Chapter 5

World Higher Education Database www.whed.net
International Association of Universities https://iau-aiu.net
United World Colleges www.uwc.org
The Indigenous Collective
www.theindigenouscollective.org
Indigenous Scholars Network
http://raveninstitute.ca/indigenous-scholars-network
ICC Alaska https://iccalaska.org
Te Mana Raraunga (The Māori Data Sovereignty Network)
www.temanararaunga.maori.nz
Chicago Latinx Collective
https://chicagolatinxscholars.com
Black Doctoral Network
https://blackphdnetwork.wildapricot.org
LGBT Consortium www.lgbtconsortium.org.uk

Chapter 4

Additionally, see the end of Chapter 4 for Disability networks.

Legal advice

If you are experiencing bullying, discrimination, or other unfair or illegal practices within study or work, you should consider legal advice. This may be something available via your union or professional organisation, or you could find a solicitor or lawyer that specialises in workplace or academic disputes. Many people I've spoken with are afraid to seek the legal help they're entitled to due to a fear of costs, but some lawyers will see you for a short period for free. Always confirm this in advance so you are not unexpectedly billed. Some solicitors and volunteer groups offer free advice – use your social networks to locate them. You may not need to pay until your case is resolved and, if you are successful, it may be that the costs will be met by your institution/employer. Crowdfunding can also help if you are struggling financially and need legal or medical help.

Chapters 3 and 5

Support groups

Support groups can be accessed online, via email, social media and telephone (including freephone/toll free numbers). They can help with academic issues, financial worries, human rights, relationship problems, bereavement, provide help for parents or carers, help with illness awareness, or provide information on survivor groups, to name just a few. These can be spaces where you share with others who know what you are going through and can give different perspectives and practical advice, encouragement and reassurance.

Chapters 5–6

Become a befriender

If you're wanting to overcome loneliness or help others there are a number of ways to build connections. Projects others in academia have tried include:

Befriending schemes – where staff and students reach out to each other or to the wider community.

Afternoon tea – taking turns to host isolated members from your community who might appreciate some company with schemes like Re-engage www.reengage.org.uk

Gig buddies – this is a UK scheme that is being extended in different countries where volunteers are paired with autistic or learning disabled fans of music, comedy, film or theatre, which you can enjoy together: www.gigbuddies.org.uk

Readers – this might include recording newspapers and audio books for blind or partially sighted community members (www.tnauk.org.uk); reading to older people (ask your nearest residential home if they're interested); listening to school children and adult language learners read (http://rva.org.uk/volunteering); or reading aloud to pets in need of rehoming in animal shelters.

Care homes – either making time for students or staff to visit residents, or where students may live within a facility at a reduced rent in exchange for supporting older housemates.

Pen friends – these may be via letter, email, Skype or Facebook and can connect students with peers in other colleges or countries, or connect you with isolated individuals through schemes like Silver Letters (www.thesilverline.org.uk), which connects you with an elderly individual, or Letter Link (https:// prisonfellowship.org.uk/our-work/letter-link), which connects you with a prisoner, including connections for prisoners undertaking degrees. These schemes exist in many countries, but look for a regulated charity to ensure you're supported in your support of others.

Host families – offering a place to visit for overseas students and staff, refugee academics, care leavers, and estranged students and staff. This might be an occasional meet up or a place to stay over the holidays. Some of these roles are voluntary, while others are paid for via exchange programmes. Many universities organise host schemes, or you can search for host family advertisements in your country.

Depending on where you are located you may need to be trained and vetted prior to taking on these roles and will need to commit to them for some time in order to support those you'll be befriending.

Your doctor

Your General Practitioner (GP)/Family Doctor can help with general health and if you are exhibiting stress or other concerning symptoms. Before you see your doctor it's a good idea to take your own medical history. Use the questions in the *Your medical history* checklist to inform appointments.

Chapter 6

Your medical history

- How old are you?
- How would you describe your sexuality? (E.g. straight, gay, bi, queer, questioning, asexual, man who has sex with men.)
- Do you have any questions or worries about your sexuality?
- What's your gender? (E.g. woman, trans woman, gender queer/non-conforming.)
- Is your gender presenting any worries or concerns for you?
- What ethnic group are you from?
- Is racism affecting your mental or physical wellbeing?
- Are you disabled?
- What assistance might help you? Is ableism affecting your daily life?
- What's your relationship status at the moment? (E.g. single; dating (one person or several); in a relationship (open or closed); cohabiting or married (including open/closed marriages); separated or divorced; widowed.) Are you experiencing any relationship problems? (E.g. relationship violence, family worries, psychosexual difficulties, arguments.)
- How is your physical health? Do you have any diagnosed physical health conditions? Any symptoms you'd like to talk about?
- What is your mental health like? Do you have any diagnosed mental health problems? Any symptoms that are troubling you?

- Are you taking any medication at the moment (including supplements or products you've self-prescribed/bought yourself)?
- If you are a smoker how much do you smoke per day? Do you smoke cigarettes or vape?
- If you drink alcohol, how much alcohol do you drink per week on average?
- Do you take any recreational drugs?
- Are you working? Describe your job and any issues related to it. If you're unemployed, how long has this been the case and are there any issues relating to unemployment, accessing benefits or finances that are troubling you?
- Are you studying? How is that going?
- What, if anything, makes your problems/symptoms/situation worse or better?
- Are there any causes you can think of that might be partly or wholly responsible for your current problems? (E.g. past or recent abuse, racism, pre-existing health conditions, disability, workplace bullying, poverty, family difficulties or carer responsibilities.)

You can show these answers to a nurse, doctor or therapist if it's easier than talking.

If you found this challenging you don't have to tell your employer why you are seeing the doctor, but if organising seeing the doctor alongside your work is difficult then talk to the receptionist at the doctors to see what they can do to help. If it means you have to use holiday or spare time to see the doctor, use that even if it's less than ideal (and unfair). Your health comes first. Depending on your location you can ask to see a woman or man doctor, or have a chaperone or interpreter. You can refuse medical students if you don't wish them to be present. You can see your doctor alone or with a friend, partner or advocate. They can wait outside for you or come in if you need assistance with interpreting, dressing, mobility or remembering. Your doctor can intervene with sick notes if you need time off or note how work has made you unwell. Those aged under 25 may be able to access young people's services, and some health centres offer men- or women-only clinics. The doctor should treat you compassionately and confidentially so it's important to be as frank as possible. If you are scared any information you disclose will be used against you, speak to a charity that understands your issues prior to seeking medical advice, as they can explain how best to proceed (see Chapter 6 for different charities that could assist you). There's more information on preparing to see your doctor here: www.nhs.uk/using-the-nhs/nhs-services/gps/what-to-ask-your-doctor.

Chapter 6

Therapy

You may see a therapist alone or with a partner or your family (with the consent of all involved. Please note partner or family therapy is not recommended in abusive situations). Therapists can cover a variety of subjects. Some may be referred via your doctor, or you might access them through a university or other workplace. Sometimes organisations bring in therapists if there has been a traumatic event or widely reported student/staff distress. You can also pay for a therapist privately, with some offering a sliding fee scale, and some charities offer free support and sessions.

You can find a UK therapist via www.bacp.co.uk (search within your area and look for practitioners qualified to offer therapy on psychosexual and relationship problems). Details of therapists in other countries can be found via the European Association for Psychotherapy www.europsyche.org, the World Council for Psychotherapy www.worldpsyche.org. You can also try Better Help www.betterhelp.com for other resources.

Therapists can see clients in person, or talk on the phone or online (e.g. Skype, email). You can decide which format is the most accessible for you. Talk to different therapists before committing to one you feel comfortable with and who can meet any accessibility requirements you have (wheelchair access, interpreters etc).

Therapy sessions are usually time limited – for example 40 minutes to an hour of a face-to-face/phone/ video consultation, or a set period of time to exchange emails back and forth. The therapist may decide with you how many sessions you need before you begin, and that may be reviewed as you progress through therapy. The therapist will take a similar history to one a doctor would (see above) and ask what you hope to gain from therapy. You should feel able to ask your therapist what they are doing and why at any time, and tell them if you feel uncomfortable or upset. Your therapist isn't there to fix or save you, but you should feel heard, respected and empowered throughout. You may feel a mix of emotions after therapy, which is worth feeding back to your therapist. As is having time to rest, recover and reflect, or to switch off after your session with some of the activities listed in Chapter 7. Find out more on what to expect from therapy here: www.itsgoodtotalk. org.uk/useful-resources.

Life coach

Life coaches are particularly useful if you wish to revaluate your life, establish routines, get more organised, reflect on your current situation, set goals or make plans to change your current life path. You can engage them for a period of time and have face-to-face or online sessions, establishing what you want to achieve, setting goals, working towards targets and noting where you want to change. Coaches cannot give medical or therapeutic advice but if you are struggling with feeling overwhelmed or uncertain about the future, or with building your confidence, they are ideal. Gary Wood provides an excellent overview of how coaching works and what to look for when selecting a coach www.drgarywood.co.uk.

Other support people have found useful

Cleaner	Typist
Laundry service	Foodbank
Childminder	CV/Job Coach
Hairdresser	Proofreader/Editor
Beautician	Accountant
The gym and/or personal trainer	Careers Advisor/Coach
	Occupational Therapist

Who else can you add to your support network that isn't listed here?

Treat yourself as well as you do your phone

Whenever I tell people in workshops they treat their phones better than they do themselves, there's always laughter – and disbelief. But when they tell me how they look after their phones they say:

Put a cover on it. Insure it. Password protect it. Ensure updates are installed. Never let the battery go flat. Check in with it first thing in the morning and last thing at night. Give it several hours of attention per day.

You DO treat your phone better than yourself!

What if you were to give yourself the same amount of care? To keep yourself safe. To have insurance and back-up plans for yourself if things go wrong? To watch your personal safety? To prioritise yourself and give yourself plenty of quality time? And to never let yourself get exhausted?

Each time you give your phone attention, put the same energy into looking after yourself.

References

Baldwin, J., Giovanni, N., 1973. *A Dialogue*. Lippincott, London.
Bannon, K., 2016. Radical Hope: A Teaching Manifesto. The Tattoed Professor. www.thetattooedprof.com/2016/07/06/radical-hope-a-teaching-manifesto.
Boynton, P., 2016. *The Research Companion: A Practical Guide for the Social Sciences, Health and Development*, 2nd ed. Routledge.
Lorde, A., 1988. *A Burst of Light: And Other Essays*. Ithaca, NY: Firebrand Books.

Werner, D., Thuman, C., Maxwell, J. ed., 1970. *Donde No Hay Doctor, First*, Hesperian Press.

Williams, R., 1989. *Resources of Hope: Culture, Democracy, Socialism*. Verso.

Williamson, M., 1992. *A Return to Love: Reflections on the Principles of A Course in Miracles*. Harper Collins.

3 Giving and receiving care

This chapter explores ways you can look after yourself and care for other people. It's common to have more than one problem at a time; for the same problem to keep repeating; to take time to extricate yourself from situations; for one set of difficulties to set off more issues; and to expect numerous problems over a lifetime. The same level of assistance may not be needed for each situation, but help-seeking isn't rationed. Just because you got help once, doesn't stop you using it again. This includes asking people to repeat, explain or note things if you've forgotten or didn't understand.

Before you can ask for help, you need to:

- Recognise you need assistance.
- Believe you are worthy of support.
- Know who you might approach for help.
- Have the confidence that if you make a request it will be honoured.

These ideas sound simple but may be difficult in practice. Therapy (see Chapter 2) and additional support (see Chapters 3 to 6) may be useful if you are not yet able to seek or accept assistance.

Remember also:

- There is NO LIMIT on how often you can seek help.
- It's sensible to have more than one place or person you can go to if you need a lot of support (as opposed to relying on one friend, colleague or family member).
- It is helpful to use of a range of individuals and organisations to get answers, reflect, find solutions and plan further actions.

How do I know I need help?

You may already recognise you need assistance, but you should seek advice and care if your worries and reactions to issues, and/or mental or physical health symptoms are:

- Causing you pain, fear, embarrassment, inconvenience or distress (or all of these).
- Intruding into or disrupting your daily life.
- Not explained by other factors (e.g. work and home life is fine but you still feel anxious or can't stop crying).
- Not relieved by things you try (e.g. taking painkillers, trying to relax, adjusting your workspace to feel more comfortable) or by things that have worked in the past.
- Getting worse or more intense, or not going away.
- Leaving you feeling like you cannot cope or will harm yourself.
- Leading you to do things that are putting you or others at risk (see below), or leaving you feeling out of control or otherwise vulnerable.
- Making other people concerned about your wellbeing, or if your actions or behaviours are causing distress or harm to others.

Chapter 1,
pp. 25–29

Chapter 6

Ways to raise issues

You can ask for help in person via face-to-face group or individual meetings that may be either formal or informal; via email, text, letter, WhatsApp, Facebook, Instagram or other Social Media; or using charities or helplines. Prior to connecting with others, it may help to write or record yourself describing how you are feeling, what is going on and what help you'd like. This can be especially useful if you are too unwell or distressed to communicate what is going on, or find it less embarrassing or stigmatising to have someone read what is happening and then begin a dialogue with you on or offline.

Chapters 2
(pp. 62–63)
and 4

Conversation starters

'I am feeling/I feel ...'
'I think/I've been wondering ...'
'I've had a bad day'
'I'm worried/bothered about ...'
'I'm really struggling with ...'
'I'm not okay'
'I'm finding it hard to cope'
'I need your help with ...'
'I'd like to talk to you but I'm finding it difficult'
'I may cry/go quiet/be angry, but please bear with me'
'I'm not sure how to say this but I'm going to try'
'Please call me'
'I need a friend'

Along with the conversation starters given in the box you can identify a word, sentence or image to show you need help. If you are in particular distress you could also put a message on social media inviting others to respond, including raising the alarm if you are at risk from others (for example if you are in an abusive relationship, a date has gone wrong, or if you are in a research setting where you feel threatened or are in danger – see Chapter 5 in Boynton 2016). On that note, if you are doing any research that requires field work; shifts, unsociable hours or evening work; home visits or travel, you should establish a clear network of who you can call if you are at risk – including your colleagues and local emergency services (see Boynton 2016, pp. 167–198). Having a reporting system to record adverse events is also necessary. If you are feeling particularly distressed, depressed, depersonalised or anxious, or otherwise physically unwell you may have different needs from those outlined above and may decide to carry and share a care plan. A template for such a plan can be seen in the box below:

Chapter 4

Chapter 6

My care plan

- *I like to be referred to as ...* Your name and how to pronounce it. This might be your first name, full name or title, e.g. Ms or Dr, and your preferred pronouns.
- *I need the following accommodations ...* Note if you need an interpreter, wheelchair access, easy-read instructions etc.
- *I am taking the following medication ...* State what these are and where they can be found (e.g. in the fridge, your bag etc).

- *If I'm showing the following symptoms I need emergency care* ... List symptoms and who to call for help (e.g. your doctor, emergency services or a mental health crisis team).
- *If I have the following symptoms I don't need emergency help but I do need assistance* ... List symptoms and what people can do to help (e.g. support you to lie down).
- *It will make me worse if you* ... List what might be mentally or physically harmful or cause an adverse event.
- *I've already tried* ... Note what has already been done and doesn't need repeating or discussing.
- *I'd really like advice about* ... State if there is something you would like to be told.
- *I'm afraid/concerned about* ... Note things that are frightening you or could put you in danger.

Can anyone intervene on my behalf?

You can appoint someone to notify your work or college you will be absent if you have had an accident; are unwell (physically or mentally); have been detained or arrested; or if there has been a family/relationship crisis or bereavement. Always follow this up yourself by sharing what has happened. In some cases that may require a formal noting of events or a conversation with your colleagues, supervisor or workplace department (human resources, occupational health, lawyers) to assess your needs. It is quite common for parents, partners or friends to contact colleges and other academic workplaces with

Chapter 1,
pp. 25–29

permission. If you are seriously concerned about a friend/
colleague/student's wellbeing, particularly if they have
threatened to harm themselves or others, you may wish
to raise this with their college or workplace.

Preparing to seek help

Getting it *right* …

… Ask:

The *right* person;

at the *right* time;

in the *right* way; and

via the *right* channel.

This may seem exactly the *right* advice – perhaps you've
heard it before. But is it really useful? It's technically correct but extremely difficult to do in reality. We very often
aren't in a position to access help in stepwise ways and it
may not be available anyway. Life is messy. It's hard (and
not always desirable) to do things neatly.

   What you can do …

Chapters 4–6

1 Think about who can help you.
2 Consider ways to reach out.
3 Check when support is available and if you need to
   book any appointments.
4 Note what you want to say and ensure you've got
   available any evidence and documentation that may
   be required.

5 Ask for help and report problems sooner rather than later.

6 Make full use of allies/advocates/intermediaries.

7 Note any barriers or blocks, imposed by others or by yourself, that may be in the way of you accessing assistance.

Chapters 5 and 6

8 Understand other people have lives, limits and boundaries, so check they are in a position to assist and accept if they aren't able to help.

9 Ensure you use the appropriate channels to log incidents or request accommodations.

Chapter 4

10 If you don't feel able to report what is going on, at least let *someone* know if you are in crisis.

11 If things are resolved, cancel any support already offered. Equally, if you feel provided support is not helping it's okay to refuse. This means others waiting for help can then access it.

Chapter 4

12 Take notes, record meetings or ask a friend/colleague/union rep to assist.

Chapters 4 and 5

13 Accept invitations! If someone asks how you're doing and you'd appreciate their support, *say if you are not okay*.

Help! I can't accept help

It is okay to ignore, reject or question advice you are unsure about, or to adapt it to suit your needs or situation if the advice is counterproductive or harmful (for example, someone encouraging you to give up essential medication).

Chapter 1

It may not mean you are wrong, but it might be the advice is wrong **for you**. Why? Because it:

- Is too expensive.
- Is designed for people that are WEIRD (white, western, educated, from industrialised, rich, democratic societies) (Henrich et al. 2010).
- Is presented in a format you cannot access or understand.
- Assumes you're at fault for rejecting or questioning the model of advice offered.
- Does not suit your culture, faith or political ideals.
- Isn't feasible given your immediate circumstances (for example someone in a violent relationship with other dependents being told to 'just leave').
- Isn't designed to help you make any meaningful change.

However, you may be unable to accept help for other reasons, such as:

- When you previously tried to get help it wasn't available.
- Past experiences of abuse, abandonment or rejection makes it difficult to trust any help offered.
- You fear change.
- Opportunities/choices/options are limited, leaving you unsure how to enact any advice offered.
- Low confidence and esteem issues mean you don't believe you can make any changes.
- You're scared it will make things worse.
- You've been threatened by someone.
- You want someone else to come and change things or save you.
- You're so traumatised and/or exhausted by everyday racism, sexism, ableism, LGBTQ+ phobia, poverty, precarity, health problems or bullying/abuse that even simple decisions feel impossible to make.
- You're from a country or culture where accessing services is taboo, difficult or impossible; or you have relocated and are not aware you could now benefit from services more easily.

- You know systems and services are designed to keep you out, or are a risk to you.
- You think 'what's the point?' or 'it'll never work', meaning you don't try or are quick to accept failure.

Making use of 'Unrecovery'

As already mentioned in Chapter 1, much self-help advice is based on the assumption that people have a lot of agency and are able to change their circumstances with relative ease. This underpins many messages of resilience or change that encourage us to 'recover' from our problems and adversities while ignoring underlying structural factors outside of our control. Recovery In The Bin (RITB) is a collective of mental health survivors who have created the 'Unrecovery Star', reproduced with permission in Figure 3.1. As you can see the arms of the star each represent a different factor that will potentially cause, or worsen, your mental and physical health, or affect your personal safety and other life opportunities. Being aware of these factors may be more useful in Chapters 4–6 explaining why you may be struggling, rather than assuming you are either the cause of your difficulties or the only person that can change your circumstances. It also acknowledges how many of our problems arise from multiple sources, including wider society, families, workplaces and relationships. As such it's a tool for Chapter 1 both resisting individualised models of self-care, and highlighting societal barriers and injustices. More information on how the star was created and how it can be used can be found here:
https://recoveryinthebin.org/unrecovery-star-2.

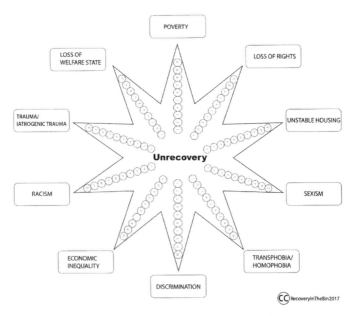

Figure 3.1 The Unrecovery Star created by service users and survivors for Recovery In The Bin.

Keep trying!

It may be that the first time you seek help you don't get what you want – the helpline might be engaged; your email request may not be immediately answered; you may be rebuffed, being told your condition or situation isn't severe enough; or you may even be made to feel you are being unreasonable. A friend or family member you hoped might assist may have troubles of their own. Being patient and persistent can feel stressful but can pay off, and if one place won't help you, keep trying others. For example, I found asking colleagues to support me as a witness to malpractice at work didn't lead to anything, but conversations with friends outside work gave me the strength to speak to a solicitor – and that sorted things swiftly. You'll note there are many self-help recommendations in this book and doubtless you'll find others if you are seeking assistance; Martin Meadows' book *How to Help Yourself with Self Help* (2019), Meadows Publishing, may make help-seeking easier to navigate.

The Kvetching Circle

'Ring Theory' was designed by Susan Silk and Barry Goldman in 2013 to help people locate themselves in difficult times. Imagine a circle. If you are the person in crisis you are at the centre. If you are not in crisis you will be in one of the rings around the centre. The closer you are to the crisis, or the person in crisis, the closer your ring will be to the centre. You can name people in these different rings so you know who is involved, where. Help and care is shared from the outermost ring to the person in the centre, distress is shared from the centre person outwards – Comfort *In*, Dump *Out*. This is called the 'Kvetching Order', where the person in the centre can offload to anyone. Others in the circle can also offload but only to those who're in the next ring outside of them. The goal here is for the person in crisis to get the support they need without having to care for others too, while those offering help can also get care but from people not so immediately impacted by a situation. Compare this with the *Ripples* exercise in Chapter 2 to see who's in your support network and where support is being shared inwards or outwards.

How to help a friend

Alongside supporting yourself, you may need to help others. Here are suggestions other people have shared on how they do this.

Listen – let them cry, or simply sit silently together. Give them space to express themselves with no correction or interruption. If there's anything they specifically do/don't want you to do, honour that (for example if they say 'I need some space to grieve', don't turn up on their doorstep).

Ask questions – how are you doing? Are you okay? Can I help? How are you feeling? What are you thinking right now? You can open up conversations with phrases like 'have you got time to talk?', 'I'm listening', 'that sounds really difficult', 'is there anything you want to share?', 'what is troubling you?'.

Show up – on or offline, let them know you are there during or immediately after a crisis, and beyond (especially months down the line when other support and recognition might have dwindled).

Give practical support – make hot drinks, bring food, offer to take over laundry, childcare, housework, shopping or other chores. Always check what they want/need before you act.

Be sensitive to their circumstances – e.g. don't bring lots of batch-cooked food if they don't have a freezer.

If you're sick, keep away! – going to work/study when you're infectious won't help your recovery and could harm others who are immunosuppressed (or just don't want your bugs).

Avoid competition – their problems are not a threat to yours, nor an invitation for you to talk about what happened to you in similar, or different, situations.

Keep confidences – if they tell you things that are private do not disclose them to others unless you feel they are in danger.

Chapter 1, pp. 25–29

Share any useful resources you feel may help them.

Don't take over – for example, don't book appointments or make complaints (unless they've asked you to advocate for them).

Be clear on your boundaries – with others and with yourself. Do not take on more than your time, energy and finances permit, and clearly communicate what help you can reasonably offer. Update if/when this changes.

Ensure you care for yourself while caring for others – prioritise rest, recuperation and self-care. If you sometimes need time out/away for respite, schedule it in.

Chapter 7

If you are already struggling with your own issues – focus on those before taking on other people's problems.

Chapter 6

If someone doesn't want help – don't be offended, challenge them, or continue to push unwanted advice or interventions (e.g. offering prayers for an atheist friend).

Not everyone knows what you do – solutions are not always obvious to others and they may have no idea about a particular situation. Offer information if asked, but don't berate them for not being where you're at.

Don't tag people into messages or share images with them of abuse, violence or prejudiced behaviour unless they have specifically asked. Marginalised groups already live with harm and don't need reminding.

There is no 'correct' way to handle shock, grief, trauma or ill health. Others may not react as you have, or as you think you would, and that's okay.

Chapter 6

Educate yourself – if they're experiencing things you're concerned over but do not know much about or haven't experienced, don't expect them to educate you. You can learn privately about health issues, sexism, racism, ableism, being LGBTQ+ etc and use this to be more empathic, rather than starting debates or discussions about their lives or expecting them to justify themselves to you.

Chapter 5

Challenge your assumptions – you may have absorbed many prejudices during your lifetime that can have a huge impact on how you interact with friends or colleagues. If you are told or feel you need to work on this, again take time to educate yourself, but don't expect your friend or colleague to teach you.

There may be things you have in common, and other things you cannot comprehend – instead of saying you know how it *is*, it's okay to say you know how it *isn't*.

You don't have to be the sole source of help – if other friends or colleagues are available you can ensure you're all offering what's needed, aren't overbearing and are avoiding any drama within the group while supporting each other.

If a friend or colleague is exiting a difficult situation – workplace abuse, a violent relationship, exploitative friendship or toxic family, it may take time and require many attempts to start taking action or get away. And they may return more than once before finally leaving. Being there, encouraging them to keep going and to take advice from charities to support them is important.

Chapters 5–6

Create safe spaces – these may be quiet or private locations where people can decompress or discuss confidential issues, or you could establish environments where people feel supported to work/study.

Establish a Sanctuary Campus – offering refuge to students or staff that are undocumented immigrants, forced migrants and asylum seekers (Bloom 2013; Bloom and Farragher 2013).

Keep reinforcing messages of a person's value, importance and right to be safe.

Some issues are not easily fixed nor need solving – the person you are supporting may need to go through it, not have it mended by you or anyone else.

Remember you will make mistakes, say and do the wrong thing and mess up – you can apologise and start over.

You'll need to adapt your support over time – what someone needs immediately following an accident/trauma/other situation will not be what is required 6–12 months later.

All of us have different preferences to receive help – it's okay to ask if you are giving what is needed and amend as appropriate.

Chapter 1, p. 19

People in distress can be upset, angry or act out of character – allow them to react as they need. It does not reflect on you. Take time away if you need it, remembering nobody should tolerate abuse, see later in this chapter for more on this.

Lots of situations are really bad – something your friend or colleague is fully aware of. While many of us get comfort from an upfront 'that sucks' when we share how we're feeling, telling us how shocking it is may not bring comfort – not least if what has shocked us is of no surprise to our friend/colleague living within hostile, prejudiced or painful situations, or if our reactions appear judgemental or disgusted.

You can't solve every problem or rescue every person – while listening and offering to be an advocate or ally is important, there may be situations where you should step away so others who are more appropriately qualified can assist.

It's their responsibility to move things forward – encourage them to help themselves.

Having looked at this list, can you spot ways that might help you too? You can adapt it from what you'd do for someone else to what would best support you.

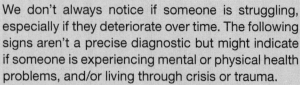

How to spot if a friend or colleague is in crisis

Chapter 6

We don't always notice if someone is struggling, especially if they deteriorate over time. The following signs aren't a precise diagnostic but might indicate if someone is experiencing mental or physical health problems, and/or living through crisis or trauma.

Talking or acting as if everything is hopeless – this may include saying they feel there's little point in doing anything or not putting any effort into activities (particularly ones they previously enjoyed or took pride in).

Isolating themselves – withdrawing from social occasions and events, dropping previously enjoyed hobbies, not keeping in touch, ignoring calls, unexplained absences, or missing classes and other deadlines.

A lack of self-care – for example not bathing or brushing their teeth for extended periods of time; increased body odour; wearing dirty clothes or looking dishevelled.

Struggling with everyday tasks – things like making meals, cleaning or getting to work may be too much for them.

A change in mood – where someone can seem like a different person. That might include being very quiet when previously they were outgoing, or manic when usually they are calm. Sometimes they may swing between highs and lows or express views that previously would have been abhorrent to them.

Appearing very anxious or agitated – this may include crying, shouting, shaking or pacing/being unable to stay still. Your friend might also destroy things they or other people value (for example breaking a valuable possession).

Hurting themselves or others – for example acting in abusive or aggressive ways; self-harming; increasing the amount they smoke; or misusing drugs or alcohol.

Changes in appetite, sleep or concentration.

Being suspicious or paranoid about others around them (without having any cause for this).

If you spot one or more of these changes, ask if your friend is okay and whether they need your help. You can also draw on the #SafetyPlan outlined in Chapter 1 and the mental health information covered in Chapter 6. You may also find these pointers enable you to see your own problems more clearly.

Be an active bystander

As discussed in Chapter 1 there are many problems in academia, meaning many of us may experience or witness one or more of the following:

Examples of unacceptable actions and behaviour

- Bullying, abuse, harassment.
- Racism, ableism, classism, LGBTQ+ phobia.
- #AntiIndigenous, #AntiSemitic or #Islamophobic actions and abuse.
- All male #Manel or all white #Wanel conference panels or other event line-ups.
- Minorities being spoken over or passed by for opportunities, including promotions, pay raises or other study/work activities.
- Excluding people on the basis of their age/gender/sexuality/race/ability/health/faith.
- Making other people feel uncomfortable or belittled with sighs, eye rolls or other negative comments.
- Asking intrusive questions about people's race, religion, disability, sexuality, income or gender – and continuing when asked to stop.
- Unwanted touching or staring and/or comments about people's physical appearance.
- #Gaslighting (telling people something has not happened when it has) or suggesting they are oversensitive or mad when appropriately responding to abuse.
- Lying to cover abuse, negligence and misde-meanours, or fabricating stories about others.
- Spreading rumours and breaching confidentiality (also known as 'badmouthing').
- Name calling.
- #Microaggressions (e.g. repeatedly mispro-nouncing names; asking a Person of Colour

where they are from; telling people with hidden disabilities or chronic illnesses they are not disabled or don't look sick; telling minorities how inspirational you find them or reacting as if they are less intelligent, criminal or don't belong).
- Shouting and yelling at people.*
- Mocking or mimicking people's accents, mannerisms, stims, tics or other habits.
- Drawing attention to things that make people feel anxious or unwelcome – for example telling someone to stop stimming, making a fuss over someone who wants to breastfeed or complaining a woman is wearing a hijab.
- Standing over people, restraining people or otherwise crowding or preventing their escape.*
- Publicly humiliating people.
- Making abusive or prejudiced 'jokes' that aren't welcome or appropriate.
- Displaying posters that objectify, sexualise, ridicule or encourage threats to harm.
- Intruding into people's personal lives (e.g. repeated calls to someone's home after work, interrupting annual leave, relentlessly monitoring private social media accounts, visiting a colleague's home uninvited).
- Removing areas of responsibility with no discussion or support.
- Supervisors/managers being absent for long periods; being overly invested/interfering; giving inconsistent instructions; showing favouritism; or plagiarising/taking credit for work that is not theirs.

- Cutting work hours or pay or ending contracts instead of implementing work-/study-based assessments and related accommodations.
- Threats to harm people or property (also known as 'Retaliation Culture').
- Punishing trivial mistakes or not allowing people to move on afterwards by constantly reminding them of something they did wrong.
- Setting people up to fail.
- Physical assault.*
- Sexual assault.
- Forcing people to do tasks that make them unsafe (for example pressuring you to have a public social media profile when you are at risk from stalking).
- Carrying out theft, blackmail, fraud, cheating and fabrication, and/or pressuring others to do so.
- Sabotaging people's work or reputations – or making threats to do so.
- Deliberately violating ethical standards and/or forcing others to do the same.
- Strategically ignoring or side-lining people, or encouraging others to do the same.
- Using email and/or social media to belittle, target, stalk or otherwise threaten targets.
- Disrupting conferences or other events on or offline with threats, mobbing, trolling or other actions designed to alarm or threaten.
- Forcing people to overwork, creating unreasonable workloads, refusing to allow leave to be taken.
- Encouraging mobbing or ganging up (where others are brought in to pick on or isolate an individual on or offline).

- Doxxing (finding out personal information about individuals and sharing online so others can use it to threaten or attack).
- Rotating targets so different individuals are picked on at different times, making it difficult for people to stick together or support the current victim.
- Overseeing unfair contracts (zero hours, unpaid work, pay inequalities).
- Not providing essential equipment, training or safe working conditions.
- Blaming others when adverse events happen that are not their fault.
- Refusing to put protocols in place to keep people safe (for example if a far right group targets an academic, the institution distancing themselves and complaining the academic has brought the institution into disrepute).

* Excluding self-defence.

If you are studying or working in an environment where one or more of the above issues are regular occurrences you may want to take action but not know how. If you're a victim you should document abuse by keeping records, asking for witnesses and collating evidence, while using your support network, taking union and legal advice, and if necessary, reporting to an ethics committee, professional body, campus security, human resources or the police. Witnesses can also do this, alongside trying the following ways to support others while keeping themselves safe.

Chapter 2

Chapters 4-6

Learn your ABCs

If you witness any of the problems described above you can:

A	B	C
ASSESS the situation	**BE** in a group	**CARE** for the victim and **CHECK** they are okay
Pay attention to what is going on, your surroundings, escape routes or any other points of danger or support. Always be mindful of your own safety and try to avoid being injured or attacked.	More people mean more opportunities to help victims, provide corroborating witness statements and take different actions to ensure the right help is delivered. If you are alone, call for help on your phone or shout 'I need help!' or 'fire!'.	Are they indicating either verbally or non-verbally that they need help? Are you aware they are in danger even if they don't appear to have noticed? Ask them 'are you okay?', 'do you need help?'. Check what they need; offer to assist them to a place of safety; sit with them until help comes; call for help, or offer other care (e.g. getting them a drink or keeping them warm).

(Adapted from *Bringing in the Bystander* by www.soteriasolutions.org/college)

In addition to your ABCs you can also implement the 4Ds.

The 4Ds

These are established *Bystander Intervention Strategies* designed to protect other people's safety and wellbeing.

Take **DIRECT ACTION** – calling out antisocial behaviour, bullying or abuse; checking the victim is okay; telling the abuser to stop. Keep calm as you do this and state what you have seen rather than your opinions. Try 'Do you need my help?' or 'shall we go over here?' – to the victim and 'Please stop shouting, it sounds very aggressive' – to the abuser. If it's safe you may want to record what is happening on your phone (audio or visually), or make notes about what you saw as soon as you are able. Be ready to share this evidence as a witness. Respect how people are coping, so if it seems they're in control you can still be present in case they need you while allowing them to deal with the situation without you correcting them. Your aim is to keep calm and keep another person safe, rather than escalating the situation or increasing the risk of harm to the victim or yourself.	Try **DISTRACTION** techniques. Begin a very general and mundane conversation that shows the victim they are supported and puts a barrier between them and any threat. You could also use your own body to put space between the victim and abuser if it does not place you at risk. Or you could tell the abuser or victim there's a phone call for one of them, or they need to come away and attend to another issue. Assess how the person is interacting with the abuser and whether they need your help. Suggest ways they can exit the situation should they wish, without assuming they need to be removed by you.

(Continued)

It may be you are already vulnerable or feel you won't be able to intervene effectively, in which case you can **DELEGATE** to a friend/colleague who you feel will have more success in handling the situation. This could also include calling campus/ workplace security, other colleagues, emergency services (if it won't exacerbate harm to the victim), or at conferences speaking to named staff that can help you if you feel threatened or are anxious about another person's wellbeing. If there is more than one of you present you might all attempt to move with the victim to a place of safety.

It may be so dangerous you cannot act to help a victim, in which case there will be a **DELAY** in the support you can offer. If you have to run away or leave the victim temporarily while you call for help, come back when it's safe to do so to see if they're okay. You can be a witness after an event, so ensure abuse/harm is recorded even if you couldn't help at the time and even if it happened some while ago.

Add *two more Ds*. Make a distinction between **discomfort** – where you could act to help another person but you choose not to because it would leave you feeling uncomfortable and awkward; and **danger** – when you or the victim are at direct risk of physical assault, injury or accident (in which case it's sensible to use the 4Ds above). Note if you're making excuses not to assist another person by deliberately confusing discomfort and danger.

Chapter 5

Many institutions now offer Active Bystander training or courses addressing the issues listed above. These may be helpful in putting these ideas into action in a high-pressured, real-life situation, which is more difficult and unpredictable than just reading about it here. Be wary of organisations providing this training with no other structural changes or support – effectively leaving students and staff to de-escalate and patrol difficult and dangerous situations.

Essentials box

Many students and staff struggling financially will not admit to it due to shame and stigma. You can create an 'essentials box' left in an accessible, private space. Get those that can afford it to donate soap/shower gel and deodorant (including unscented products), sunscreen, tights/pantyhose, sanitary towels and tampons, pens, tissues, pre-wrapped biscuits etc. Write 'help yourself' on the side and replenish when empty. In some departments/workplaces I've seen a mini foodbank in operation where people can donate tinned foods, cereals, biscuits, UHT milk, tea, coffee and other products.
www.theresearchcompanion.com/essentialsbox

Start *somewhere* with *something*

If you are struggling, unhappy and wish for things to change, at some point you need to get going. You could try making a list of what is troubling you then prioritise these things by what you can fix quickly or easily, feel most inclined to address, are able to afford, or know you have to deal with to prevent things worsening. Or you may start with something at random. The former may suit you if you have lots to deal with or prefer order; the latter if there is a lot going on but you don't feel any one thing needs prioritising. It's normal to feel unsettled and over-whelmed if you're facing many issues and/or deciding to accept help or pursue treatment. Remember, you do not have to fix everything at once. Some things can be left and may even end up being discarded. Many things will sort themselves out, whatever you do. And some things, particularly related to your health and safety, must never be ignored.

Chapters 4–6

Find out more

Practical help for you and your community in frightening and dangerous times: https://nostartoguideme.com/practical-help-in-frightening-and-dangerous-times

How to deliver Psychological First Aid
http://nostartoguideme.com/psychological-first-aid

Mental Health First Aid (MHFA) England
https://mhfaengland.org

The John Hopkins Guide to Psychological First Aid. George S. Everly Jr and Jeffrey M. Lating (2017), John Hopkins University Press.

Creative Coalitions – A Handbook for Change. Nick Martlew (2017), Crisis Action, downloadable from www.crisisaction.org

Mental Health Hotlines Worldwide (includes tips on seeking help):

Global Mental Health Resources

https://checkpointorg.com/global

Find a Helpline (UK) https://helplines.org/helplines

Make a bravery box

You will need:

- A small card or wooden box with a lid.
- Buttons of different colours, sizes and textures.
- PVA glue.

Select a few of the buttons you like best and glue them on the lid of the box.

Keep the remaining buttons and every time you do something brave, put a button into the box.

Being 'brave' might mean coming out to colleagues, asking for help with a project or job application, having a disability assessment, getting out of bed, seeing your therapist, presenting when it makes you feel anxious, or taking the first step to leaving a violent relationship. You decide what is brave, keeping goals small and achievable, and filling the box at a pace that suits you. Other people can also give you buttons to credit you for something you may not have recognised.

References

Bloom, S.L., 2013. *Creating Sanctuary: Toward the Evolution of Sane Societies*. 2nd ed. Abingdon: Routledge.

Bloom, S.L., Farragher, B., 2013. *Restoring Sanctuary: A New Operating System for Trauma-Informed Systems of Care*. New York: OUP.

Boynton, P., 2016. *The Research Companion: A Practical Guide for the Social Sciences, Health and Development*, 2nd ed. Routledge.

Henrich, J., Heine, S.J., Norenzayan, A., 2010. The WEIRDEST People in the World? *Behavioural and Brain Sciences* 33, 61–83.

4 What help do you need?

This chapter provides a list of things you may desire, require or be entitled to (depending on your location, laws and resources) in order to navigate studying/working in academia. Not all of these will be relevant to you, or always feasible depending on where in the world you're working or studying. All have been suggested by people I've worked with as a means of making their work or studying easier and fairer. Although they are broken down into different categories you'll find many overlap or interact and it may help you to note where this applies to you.

As you work through this chapter the list below may help you to use the following sources to identify or check what you may be entitled to, or what you can expect from academic spaces:

- Your contract.
- University/employer website.
- Syllabus.
- Unions and Equality, Diversity and Inclusion officers. Chapter 2
- Charities and organisations dealing with employment law, disability, minority rights, student support, and Chapters 5 and 6 mental and physical health.
- Professional bodies covering your work/academic speciality.

- Comparisons with other organisations, institutions or countries (aka what are other people and places doing effectively?).
- Occupational health and human resources.
- Staff/student training units.
- Staff/student conduct or conflict resolution documents, guidance or officers.
- Policy documents or other guidance on managing complaints; or specific staff/departments where complaints may be made.
- Ombudsperson based within your university, organisation, state or country.
- Your support network may also be an invaluable source of information.

Chapter 2

Please remember, making disclosures about your needs and situation should only be done if you feel it will not cause you further risk or harm. Think carefully about what you disclose, to whom, and when.

As you read through the list below use the boxes provided as follows:

☑ (Tick) if you're already supported in a particular area (or know help is available even if you don't need it currently).
☒ (Cross) if this support is not offered.
☐ (Leave blank) if you are unsure if support is available or it is irrelevant to you, or shade in the box if you would *like* a specific accommodation or intervention to be available to you.

At the end of this chapter I'll ask you to revisit the following list to identify any support you have, what you need and where to find it.

Reasonable adjustments and accommodations

These are actions or interventions designed to eradicate or reduce disadvantages and barriers for disabled people, older people, parents and carers, and other minorities. Note which of the following you might need and whether it is available.

☐ Making premises for teaching, research, conferences etc easier to access and navigate throughout *all* spaces required for work/study with ramps, signposting on walls or directions on floors.
☐ Job sharing.
☐ Home working.
☐ Accommodating dietary needs (e.g. gluten or dairy free meals).
☐ Readers for meetings and exams.
☐ Note takers/scribes.
☐ Buff or other accessible colour copies of exams or booklets.
☐ Materials/documents available in braille.
☐ Easy read typefaces on handouts, websites, essays you are marking etc.
☐ Any reading/research materials, instructions or manuals made available in advance of any classes, events, talks or shifts.
☐ Online materials that work with screen readers.
☐ The ability to use computers/laptops and/or dictaphones in classes or meetings.
☐ Written instructions to follow up verbal information (and vice versa).
☐ Captioned videos and other visual learning materials.
☐ Extra time for assessments.

☐ Interpreters.

☐ Wheelchair access to all parts of a venue used plus clear public spaces, hallways, study rooms etc for those using chairs, walkers, sticks and canes to navigate safely.

☐ Service-dog-friendly spaces.

☐ Permission to bring therapy animals into work/study spaces.

☐ Adapting/amending training, research and instruction manuals and materials for diverse audiences, e.g. providing translations or easy-read versions.

☐ Explaining the needs of other staff/students to peers (e.g. how to phrase questions, give instructions or to avoid wearing perfume).

☐ Clear and regularly updated instructions on daily routines, timetables and how everyday stuff works (including anticipating unpredictability as much as possible).

☐ Acquiring or modifying equipment and furniture.

☐ Accessible toilets that include toilet spaces for women, men and gender neutral lavatories; baby changing facilities; toilets with space for a wheelchair to maneuver, grab rails, alarm pull cord, long mirrors, lower sinks and hand driers, outward opening doors, and consistent lighting. Plus facilities to empty catheters and ostomy pouches; sanpro bins; and, if appropriate, a changing bench and hoist for adults unable to use standard accessible toilets.

☐ Help with managing and understanding timetables, workload, record keeping and planning.

☐ Noting where fluorescent lighting, noise from other colleagues or within buildings, and temperature could be uncomfortable or distracting.

☐ Support mechanisms/forward planning for students/ staff with chronic, long term, fluctuating, recurrent or life-limiting illnesses.

☐ The opportunity to wear headphones to cancel noise/ reduce stress, and explanations for colleagues about how to approach someone using headphones while working or studying.

☐ Having a named, trained, visible and regularly available support worker/mentor/officer to help check and confirm work, explain instructions or prepare for changes.

☐ Accessible parking spaces close to buildings where work/study is taking place.

☐ Reducing or removing highly scented products from work/study spaces (including air fresheners, cleaning materials or scented soaps), and asking colleagues not to wear perfume.

Understanding how things work

These are strategies to help you understand your role and what is expected of you (including recognising any barriers to your ability to work/study and your own limitations).

☐ Induction – to new courses, institutions, materials and equipment.

☐ Instructions – syllabi, regulations, information on how to use equipment, workplace/campus signposts and maps, agendas.

☐ Guidance, support and time to prepare for any metrics, measures or assessments.

☐ Clear reporting structures for adverse events, problems, questions etc.

Finance

This includes information, resources and guidance to help you obtain and manage finances and funding, or navigate hardship.

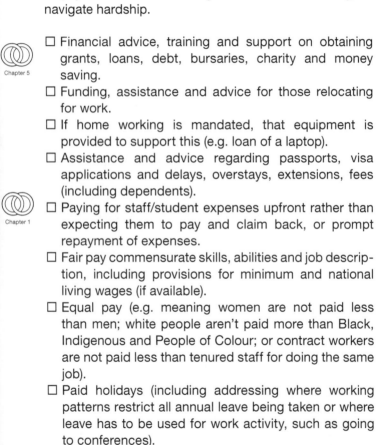

☐ Financial advice, training and support on obtaining grants, loans, debt, bursaries, charity and money saving.

Chapter 5

☐ Funding, assistance and advice for those relocating for work.

☐ If home working is mandated, that equipment is provided to support this (e.g. loan of a laptop).

☐ Assistance and advice regarding passports, visa applications and delays, overstays, extensions, fees (including dependents).

Chapter 1

☐ Paying for staff/student expenses upfront rather than expecting them to pay and claim back, or prompt repayment of expenses.

☐ Fair pay commensurate skills, abilities and job description, including provisions for minimum and national living wages (if available).

☐ Equal pay (e.g. meaning women are not paid less than men; white people aren't paid more than Black, Indigenous and People of Colour; or contract workers are not paid less than tenured staff for doing the same job).

☐ Paid holidays (including addressing where working patterns restrict all annual leave being taken or where leave has to be used for work activity, such as going to conferences).

☐ Contracts that clearly and accurately specify work/study terms, conditions and pay, and that cannot be altered without consultation, review and official amendments.

☐ Clearly stated working hours, with no open limit on hours worked (for many full-time academic staff hours are around 37+ per week, with the expectation considerably more are worked unpaid).

☐ Workplace benefits, such as pension scheme, health insurance, healthcare/checks, counseling services.

☐ Sick pay.

☐ Paid overtime that is clearly stated and honoured.

☐ Accessible and affordable transport for work and study events (plus information about public transportation routes, travel cards, conference bursaries, travel/petrol expenses; and options of using a car/taxi service if required for safer research visits or support if disabled or chronically unwell).

Health, safety, rights and wellbeing

These are adjustments and solutions that make work/study spaces more comfortable, accountable, secure and inclusive.

☐ Designated quiet spaces for privacy, decompression, breastfeeding, counseling, prayer etc.

☐ Time for lunch and tea breaks (and a culture of taking said breaks).

☐ Meal vouchers or subsidised meals.

☐ Planning and ongoing feedback to reduce risks and avoid accidents, injury or harm.

☐ Acknowledging and acting upon extenuating circumstances affecting exams, assessments, performance and wellbeing.

☐ Occupational Health Service (or equivalent) offering interventions like psychological support, uniforms, workplace training, accessibility checks and other reasonable adjustments (see above).

☐ Clear, enforced policies against bullying, harassment and abuse, and opposed to zero hours contracts and precarity.
Chapters
3 and 5

Chapters
3 and 6
☐ Student/staff representatives trained to provide Mental and Physical First Aid, and advice for minorities (e.g. women's officer, First Nations student/staff representative).

☐ Clearly identified and implemented equality and diversity policies.

☐ Access to fully functioning and modern equipment essential to work/study (e.g. mobile phones, books, weather-/site-appropriate workwear that may be paid for or subsidised).

☐ Travel and cultural advice on safe and respectful conduct for staff/students working in different cultural/country settings.

☐ Avoiding building campuses or offices or running programmes in locations where minorities may be at risk (particularly women, BIPOC, disabled, LGBTQ+, or religious students and staff). Nor requiring staff to hide their faith, sexuality or gender, or mask their disability in order to avoid harm from others.

☐ Monitoring of companies providing externally contracted employees to ensure their rights are respected and working conditions are safe.

☐ Vetting of contractors, trainers and consultants operating within academic spaces to ensure their work is current, accurate, accessible, responsive and civil (e.g. avoiding trainers that push overworking as a norm; contractors who make sexist, ableist or racist remarks; or who enter student accommodation without notice and permission).

☐ If any risks are possible from study or work (e.g. handling hazardous materials, working with cleaning products, encountering potentially distressing or dangerous situations), explaining those risks, implementing safeguarding procedures (e.g. providing phones, immunisation, safety workwear or drivers) and offering additional assistance where risky situations will be unavoidable (e.g. debriefing and/or counseling following emotional interviews).

☐ Clear safety procedures (including fire drills, lockdowns and workplace risk assessments) so everyone knows what is available and expected and can raise additional concerns or problems, and note when existing plans do not currently accommodate their needs (e.g. a safety evacuation policy that hasn't accounted for disabled students/staff).

Time out/off

We are all entitled to breaks and clear down-time where work/study does not intrude. This includes:

☐ Study leave – including taking short courses, having time away from your degree programme or taking a sabbatical.

☐ Shifting work schedules from full to part time, and vice versa.

☐ Extensions for essays, courses, upgrades, projects etc.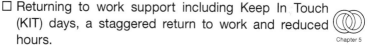

Chapter 5

☐ Respecting cultural traditions and faith holidays.

☐ Maternity/paternity/adoption/carer leave.

☐ Returning to work support including Keep In Touch (KIT) days, a staggered return to work and reduced hours.

Chapter 5

☐ Time off for hospital appointments, physiotherapy, check-ups, surgical procedures, tests and diagnoses, counseling/therapy, disability assessments.

☐ Leave for weddings and moving house, or following a relationship breakdown or bereavement.
☐ Toilet breaks, without having to ask permission.

Training and support

Our ability to work and study isn't possible without additional guidance and instruction. This may be via direct support or supervision, training days and classes, or being signposted to online resources, books or manuals.

☐ Supervision (for students, staff and researchers).
☐ Recognition and reward for work undertaken, achievements and doing more than expected.
☐ Motivation – support, encouragement, mentoring and training.
☐ Regular reviews/progress meetings (with agendas circulated beforehand and minutes/notes shared afterwards).

☐ Support and sympathy after accidents and unforeseen events in and outside academia, plus time off, assistance, legal advice, reimbursement or compensation for injuries incurred at work.

☐ Campus-/work-based career advice (including ideas for non-academic careers and jobs outside of universities).

☐ Clearly outlined misconduct/disciplinary offences and procedures (including verbal and written warnings, panels and committees).
☐ Appeals procedures for grades, degree classifications, allegations or dismissal.

☐ No opposition to industrial action, workplace meetings and organising, plus student societies/associations and residential committees.

Chapter 3

☐ Training in self-defence, handling confrontational situations, negotiating/de-escalation skills, confidence, communication skills and assertiveness.

How did you react to the checklist above?

Were you relieved to note you've got mostly ticks and so feel well supported? Perhaps you are feeling anxious about how much isn't available? Maybe you discovered things that you might be entitled to but hadn't considered? Do you think it way too idealistic or are you laughing bitterly at what may seem irrelevant if your current situation is particularly bad?

If your place of work or study covers pretty much all the points listed above and you feel well supported you can skip the next part. If you are well supported but still feeling unhappy, Chapter 5 covers a range of issues that might be responsible for your distress. However, if you would like more opportunities and assistance but are uncertain of your rights, or certain they aren't currently covered, read on.

Note all the boxes you've left blank or shaded (those listed points you are not sure about or would like to have). It may be there are things you are entitled to that are already obtainable. The list of information sources at the start of this chapter may help you identify these so you can book yourself onto training or request changes are made.

Finally, note what is not provided (those boxes in which you have placed a cross), especially if this is adversely affecting your mental or physical health, and/or personal safety. You can, as above, request those points that are Chapter 6 not provided, although you should *never assume support does not exist without asking.* However, you may be in a workplace that is familiar across academia but that

Chapter 1

exploits and does the bare minimum to support staff. One that won't honour your requests or where you may feel too intimidated or abused to ask for such support, or are made to feel worse after seeking assistance. If this is the case you can use the tips in the *How to help yourself* section at the end of this chapter.

Academic alarm bells

Alongside the problems identified in *Active bystander* (Chapter 3), there may be other areas of concern confirmed by the list above, including:

- Making accessing help, training or resources obscure and laborious.
- Requiring you to use your own time and/or pay for support that should be provided by your place of study or work.
- Expecting you to pay for and provide your own personal protective equipment (PPE).
- Refusing to help you if you don't have a specific diagnosis or other 'proof' of problems you're experiencing.
- Encouraging you to seek help then penalising you for doing so. For example, asking staff to reveal struggles with mental health, then shortly after making them redundant.
- Applying for diversity awards that require minority students/staff to undertake additional unpaid, unrewarded and potentially upsetting activities.
- Ignoring how disability, chronic illness and mental/ physical health problems may be understood in different ways by different cultures and failing to provide culturally sensitive tuition, advice or pastoral care.

- Cutting essential services, e.g. student welfare, staff/student counseling.
- A lack of trauma-informed staff available to support those in crisis.
- Failing to maintain buildings, materials, heating/air conditioning, lighting etc, which makes it dangerous to navigate spaces or to work or study.
- Glorifying overwork, either by setting unreasonable workloads or rewarding those with hectic schedules.
- Increasing or reducing workloads unreasonably and/or expecting lots of free labour (including labeling these situations as 'work experience' or 'exposure').
- Working with outside government agencies to maintain hostile environments for refugee, asylum seeking and undocumented staff and students.
- Allowing individuals or groups to use academic spaces for talks or events that threaten or direct hate towards minorities.
- Fostering toxic, hostile and competitive working environments.
- Ignoring worker's rights and laws (e.g. refusing time off for medical appointments).
- Hosting short-term, ineffective, glossy, publicity-seeking events; vanity projects; or activities that have no sustained impact; while making no effort to ensure the wider workplace is fair, legal or supportive.
- Encouraging 'feedback' (e.g. student surveys) then not listening (so students are not helped); or failing to act on racist, sexist or otherwise abusive comments made towards staff and/or allowing them to remain on staff records.
- Pushing presenteeism (including digital surveillance of student/staff activity).

Chapter 8

If you're noting an overwhelming number of alarm bells and limited support, and you lack the strength, energy, security or power to make changes, you might be better off trying to leave where you currently are.

Your responsibilities

So far we've focused on what you need from work/study, but there are also expectations **you** need to meet. Aside from familiarising yourself with entitlements, declaring any circumstances requiring reasonable adjustments, requesting what you need to navigate work/study and challenging where this is not delivered (if safe to do so), you should also be:

- Reading the syllabus, manuals and/or any regulations.
- Checking any work/learning contracts.
- Keeping up to date with any professional development, assessments and registrations.
- Attending any shifts, lectures, meetings or other requirements you are contracted for.

Chapters
3 and 5

Chapter 6
Chapter 3

- Letting people know promptly if you cannot do a particular task or if you require time off.
- Seeking care for your mental and physical health.
- Promptly reporting any accidents, incidents or problems via the correct channels, if available.
- Keeping a log book/research diary or clocking in (this may be formally required by your supervisor, but you should keep this informally if it is not or if you are self-employed).
- Filing any receipts or other work/study documentation.
- Attending training that is offered.
- Updating skills as required.

How to help yourself

Being overwhelmed and exploited at work can leave you feeling isolated and exhausted, however, there are things you can do to stand up for your rights:

Join a union – you're always stronger collectively. Unions will offer you advice and information, support you if you need to raise a grievance, take industrial action, make a complaint, and will keep you updated on benefits and rights. Although please note that unions are not always available and may be suppressed, in which case other parts of your support network may be safer to reach out to. Chapter 2 Chapter 2

Work together with colleagues – on or offline to support each other against unfair practices and check what you're legally entitled to. This may particularly benefit you if you struggle with ordering, comprehension or staying focused. Chapter 2

Enforce your downtime and refuse to take on additional, unpaid work (see Chapter 7). This may be done formally by stating you are unable to do a particular job, or you may simply choose to ignore requests for additional labour that does not directly benefit you. Chapter 7

Weigh up the amount of additional/unpaid work you are doing to establish what you are getting versus what academia is getting. If the balance is in their favour then cut back. If you want to put in extra hours make that for your benefit, not theirs. Chapter 5

Note if you are always putting other people first – it is understandable you may want to help other colleagues or support students, but that should not come at the expense of your own health and wellbeing. Look after yourself and then think about caring for other people. Chapter 3

Chapter 6

Get signed off work/study if it is making you mentally or physically sick.

Take legal advice – either via a union or through a solicitor specialising in the rights of academic students

Chapters 2 and 3

and staff.

If there are things you need that your workplace seems unwilling to offer but that you can *go elsewhere* for (e.g. an online training course or a workshop at a conference that updates your skillset), then do go elsewhere for

Chapter 5

these. Yes, it's wrong you have to do it, but if you need something that your workplace is obstructing, bypass them rather than letting them hold you back.

Consider if the things that aren't on offer are *dealbreakers*. If your workplace largely provides what you need,

Chapters 5 and 6

you enjoy being there and you can fill in the gaps yourself, that may be easier to accept than a workplace where there are major inequalities and a toxic atmosphere.

Speak out! Increasingly people are sharing stories of unfair practices in academia on their own or on other

Chapter 2

people's social media accounts with the help of journalists, or through academic news sites or collectives. The more these are exposed the easier they are to unite against, and you will find you are not alone. Many online support networks allow you to post anonymously,

Chapters 2 and 3

helped by the administrators, where you can share what is happening and get advice. Knowing you have other people supporting you is particularly reassuring if you are working in a threatening environment, if you are unsure of your rights and responsibilities, are afraid to speak out or if you are being threatened in any way. Remember, whatever happens, you are not alone and many problems will have a solution – even if you're not able to recognise it currently.

Find out more

Below are a number of organisations people have used to learn more about their wellbeing and rights during work or study. This is not a comprehensive list and you may find searching government, university and other organisational websites reveals additional policies, training or other materials. If these don't exist you may be able to adapt some of the resources shared below and elsewhere in this book (particularly in Chapters 5 and 6) to suit your needs.

Rights, training and safety

Safety and Health Practitioner www.shponline.co.uk
Canadian Centre for Occupational Health and Safety www.ccohs.ca
Safe Work Australia www.safeworkaustralia.gov.au
European Agency for Safety and Health at Work https://osha.europa.eu/en
Employers Responsibilities (UK)
www.hse.gov.uk/workers/employers.htm
Identify your training needs
https://theresearchcompanion.com/trainingneeds
ACAS Model Workplace
https://obs.acas.org.uk/modelworkplace
Health and Safety Complaints (UK)
www.hse.gov.uk/contact/complaints.htm
Education Support Partnership (UK)
www.educationsupportpartnership.org.uk
ProtectED runs an accredited scheme to assess how UK universities are addressing student wellbeing. Downloadable resources can be found here:
www.protect-ed.org/resources with paid for materials available via their website.

Student Minds (UK) have launched a University Mental Health Charter that colleges can sign up to and identify key activities for a whole-university approach:
www.studentminds.org.uk/charter.html
O'Brien, T., Guiney, D., 2018. *Staff Wellbeing in Higher Education: A Research Study for Education Support Partnership.* www.educationsupportpartnership.org.uk/sites/default/files/staff_wellbeing_he_research.pdf
Racism, it stops with me (Australia)
https://itstopswithme.humanrights.gov.au
Runnymede Trust (UK) www.runnymedetrust.org
Equality and Human Rights Commission (UK)
www.equalityhumanrights.com/en
Anti-Racist Resources https://theresearchcompanion.com/antiracistresources
Working Families (UK) www.workingfamilies.org.uk

Chapter 5

Resources for students and staff

Higher Education Authority (UK) www.heacademy.ac.uk
Office for Students (UK) www.officeforstudents.org.uk
Tertiary Education Quality and Standards Agency Australia www.teqsa.gov.au
Quality Assurance Agency (UK) www.qaa.ac.uk
Office of the Independent Adjudicator for Higher Education (UK) www.oiahe.org.uk
European Network of Ombuds in Higher Education (ENOHE) www.enohe.net
European University Association https://eua.eu
Advance HE (UK) www.ecu.ac.uk

Disability and accessibility

Global Disability Rights Now
www.globaldisabilityrightsnow.org

Leonard Cheshire www.leonardcheshire.org
Scope www.scope.org.uk
National Autistic Society guide for supporting students in FE and HE
www.autism.org.uk/professionals/teachers/fe-he.aspx
University reasonable adjustments for autistic students undertaking a viva and other examinations:
https://soyoureautistic.com/university-reasonable-adjustments
ADD International www.add.org.uk
Chronically Academic https://chronicallyacademic.org
Welcomed and valued: supporting disabled learners in medical education and training. General Medical Council (UK). (2019)
www.gmc-uk.org/education/standards-guidance-and-curricula/guidance/welcomed-and-valued
Clarke, P., Beech, D., 2018. *Reaching the Parts of Society Universities Have Missed: A Manifesto for the New Director of Fair Access and Participation.* Paul HEPI and Brightside. www.hepi.ac.uk/wp-content/uploads/2018/05/HEPI-Brightside_WP-Manifesto-for-OfS_FINAL-Report-106.pdf

5   Threats to your wellbeing

'*Pack up your troubles in your old kit bag and smile, smile, smile*' – my grandfather used to sing if I was ever feeling a bit wobbly. This chapter's a bit like a kit bag full of troubles, listing the many worries people have shared with me about academia.

You can search this alphabetical list for key issues, or browse the whole chapter, noting what's affecting you or those you are supervising/caring for. Many of these issues overlap, intersect and interact so note links between what is covered here and elsewhere in the book for a clearer picture of your situation. For each brief entry you'll find problems people have encountered, crowdsourced solutions and, crucially, links to further information, including hashtags. It's not an exhaustive list nor presented in any order of magnitude, and not every issue will apply to you. As you work through this chapter remember the *How to help yourself* list in Chapter 4 (p. 111) while questioning who is brought in and left out, alongside taking, breaking and remaking these suggestions (Boynton 2016).

Chapter 1

A

Problem	Try
#Ableism Disabled staff and students struggle with discriminatory practices, actions, attitudes, language and beliefs that prevent people from participating in work, study and social events. They may also be infantalised or treated as inferior, which limits their potential, perpetuates inequalities and permits abuse to thrive. Ableism affects individuals with physical disabilities, those who are neurodiverse, have mental health problems, chronic or life-limiting illness and pain. It intersects with other marginalisations (race, gender, sexuality, poverty) and serves to isolate, patronise and otherwise harm.	Hearing about how bad academia is from others can scare you into assuming requests for accommodations and adjustments won't be honoured – but they may! So *always* ask. 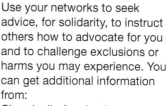 Chapter 4 Where possible remember to do this before applying for a course or job, attending an interview or going to a conference. Continue to note what you need and request it throughout any period of study or work. Use your networks to seek advice, for solidarity, to instruct others how to advocate for you and to challenge exclusions or harms you may experience. You can get additional information from: Chronically Academic https://chronicallyacademic.org Stop Ableism www.stopableism.org Dignity and Respect Campaign https://dignityandrespect.org Rooted in Rights https://rootedinrights.org Disability Visibility Project https://disabilityvisibilityproject.com

Chapters 1 and 3

(Continued)

A

Problem	Try
#Abled allies can note where there are problems and help address them through structural changes, education and support. Chapters 3 and 4	Stairway to STEM www.stairwaytostem.org/ Office for Students www.officeforstudents.org.uk/ (Search for disability.) #AskDontGrab #EverydayAbleism #AbleismInAcademia #spoonie #AutisticsInAcademia #ActuallyAutistic #AutisticCollege #disability #DisabilityAwareness #disabled #wheelchair #inclusion #SpecialNeeds #MentalHealth #autism #accessibility #DisabilityRights #DisabilityBenefits #diversity #asd #add #adhd #MentalIllness #ptsd #AutoImmuneDisease #ComingOutAsDisabled #CripTax #CripTheVote #DisabilityTooWhite #SpoonieChat
#Access This may include not being able to afford to study; being prevented from working/ studying because accommodations haven't been made; limitations due to your own physical or mental wellbeing; or Chapter 1 systems designed to keep you out.	Aside from addressing any illegalities in limiting your access turn to your networks; join support or pressure groups (e.g. Indigenous Students, Black Academics, Disabled Scholars); work for widening participation initiatives; and report barriers and blocks. Chapter 4

A

Problem	Try
Ageism Young or senior staff/ students may experience judgements about their abilities and competencies (e.g. assuming an older student is just studying to pass the time), and may potentially miss out on opportunities as a consequence (e.g. not offering jobs to older staff or refusing to let younger students lead or manage events). They may also be given things unfairly (e.g. expecting younger staff to do additional unpaid work as a 'career opportunity'. Older students may also be excluded from Early Career Researcher funding and training if it is aimed at those aged under 30.)	Early Career Blog http://earlycareerblog.blogspot.com (Noting many #ECRs aren't young.) PLOS ECR Community https://blogs.plos.org/thestudentblog *The Mature Students Handbook.* Lucinda Becker (2009), MacMillan Study Skills. *Never Too Late: A Mature Student's Guide to Going to University.* Joanne M. Weselby (2014), Create Space. #studentvoices #adultlearners

(Continued)

A

Problem	Try
#AltAc Altac (sometimes referred to as Alt-Ac or post-ac) originated in a Twitter conversation between Bethany Nowviskie and Jason Rhody about alternative academic careers. Too often anyone who'd completed a PhD and didn't work in university teaching or research were pejoratively described as 'non-academic'. This left those wanting to use their academic skills in jobs outside of teaching/research (for example in industry or administration) without adequate and positive information about jobs open to them.	Right at the start of this book I noted how 'academia' can mean many things, and it's vital to note 'academia' does not mean 'university'. You can be an academic in or outside a university; and not everyone working in a university has an academic role. Suggesting 'academic' (aka teaching and particularly research) is superior to all other jobs (in particular service or manual roles) not only creates an environment where bullying and exploitation can thrive, but it also limits career choices and affects confidence.You can learn more about AltAc careers at: AltAc Adventures https://medium.com/altac-chronicles The Professor is In – It's okay to quit https://theprofessorisin.com/its-ok-to-quit The Leveraged PhD https://theleveragedphd.com The Scholapreneur http://thescholarpreneur.com #AltAcademy #TheLeveragedPhd #postac #WithaPhd #AcademicLife #NotThatKindofDoctor #ProfessorChronicles #BeyondProf #ThisIsMe

Chapter 3

A

Problem	Try
Assessment Depending on where you are studying or working this may include a growing number of things that are in themselves stressful and may control, pressurise, bully and exclude. Students and staff have listed struggling with: essays, exams etc (see later in this chapter); observations; tests; performance-based research funding (#PBRF); internal reviews; visitation committees; targets; portfolios; evaluations; upgrades; tenure committees; Enhancement-led Institutional Review (#ELIR); impact case studies; Teaching Excellence and Student Outcomes Framework (#TEF); Research Excellence Framework (#REF); professional accreditation; compliance standards; classifications; rankings; student/staff satisfaction surveys; Excellence in	Being able to show what you have undertaken and achieved is important whatever you are working on or studying. However, the increase in assessments across academia has added to workload, stress levels and other negative outcomes. Unions are challenging the effect assessments have on staff, while support networks are helping people on a daily basis. If you are adversely affected, try looking at the resources in Chapter 6. Numerous problems are documented with the assessments described here, but if you're unable to escape assessments the following resources may help you navigate them more effectively: Research Impact Academy www.researchimpactacademy. com Fast Track Impact www.fasttrackimpact.com While these sites provide a helpful antidote and resistance: UKPUR https://ukpur.home.blog

Chapter 1, pp. 8–14

Chapter 3, pp. 85–89

(Continued)

A

Problem	Try
Research (#ERA); quality reviews/frameworks/ standards; Knowledge Exchange Framework (#KEF); and the High Council for Evaluation of Research and Higher Education (#HCRES). And if that's not enough, more struggles are being added all the time! Using this list as keywords will help you locate more critical articles and research papers to inform opposition to unfair practices.	DORA https://sfdora.org USSBriefs https://ussbriefs.com #UUKSpin #REFoff #REFRAF @precariousuni on Twitter The hastags #YesUniCan and #MadeAtUni can be used in both celebratory and ironic ways.
#Authorship Theoretically it should be simple. If you're writing a paper or report those involved should be credited fairly and transparently for the work they do. In reality? Supervisors publish their student's work or insist on having their names on papers even if their input has been minimal. 'Big names' in particular fields also demand authorship without having earned it.	Excluding people from authorship, giving authorship when it isn't earned or making people into co-authors without their consent are all unethical. With a growing number of resources aimed at showing how authorship can be earned there is no excuse not to credit authors fairly, although the culture of bullying, harassment and competition in academia makes this difficult.

A

Problem	Try
While community researchers, Early Career Researchers (ECRs) and underrepresented minorities (URMs) are frequently dropped from being authors; women in particular are affected by a lack of credit for work undertaken. This may be explained as an oversight or by downplaying the role an author had, or as a means to create alliances. Whatever the excuse, it's not fair but causes enormous stress, as can the alarming situation when work you have neither approved nor been involved with is put forward for peer review or published with your name attached. This can be a particular problem if the work is not of a high standard.	I cover a stepwise plan on gaining authorship in my book *The Research Companion* (Boynton 2016, pp. 78–79 and pp. 82–83), which includes information on what to do if involved in an authorship dispute. You can also use the following guides to identify and negotiate authorship yourself (along with information elsewhere in this book on dealing with exploitation and harm). Committee on Publication Ethics (COPE) guide to authorship https://publicationethics.org/authorship American Psychological Association's Tips for Determining Authorship Credit www.apa.org/science/leadership/students/authorship-paper International Committee of Medical Journal Editors – Defining the role of authors and contributors www.icmje.org/recommendations/browse/roles-and-responsibilities/defining-the-role-of-authors-and-contributors.html CRediT www.casrai.org/credit.html

(Continued)

B

Problem	Try
#Babyloss We may not talk openly about it but lots of us experience #miscarriage, #ectopic pregnancy, #stillbirth, Termination for Medical Reasons (#TFMR) or infant death. Yet, these subjects remain taboo, particularly in some cultures and pressured environments where revealing a pregnancy or loss may be risky and support is limited.	Increasingly students and staff are speaking out about loss, sharing their stories on social media and requiring more humane care within academic settings. If you have lost a baby you are entitled to time off for appointments, medical care, recovery, funerals or legal meetings. You can find more information on your options and rights, and on ways to care for yourself in my other book *Coping With Pregnancy Loss* (Routledge, 2018). You can also find additional resources, hashtags and support groups where you can share how you feel or get advice via https://copingwithpregnancyloss.com
Back-ups Did you hear about the woman who'd written a book and carefully saved it on her hard drive and the whole thing crashed? It was not a good day for me! Lots of us have been in the position of losing crucial information, but making backups regularly is a good means of reducing that anxiety.	There's a stepwise guide on how to make backups here: https://theresearchcompanion.com/back-up. Remember, it's not just academic work that needs saving – records, photos or other important digital information needs backing-up too.

B

Problem	Try
#Black, #Indigenous and People of Colour As described in Chapters 1 and 3, #BIPOC students and staff experience numerous barriers within academia regarding accessing places of work and study (either being held back so entry is impossible or asked to leave when rightfully there). In addition, they also face societal and structural barriers to healthcare, social support and education; a lack of respectful, secure and fair treatment within these sectors; and restricted opportunities based around racist, colonialist and anti-indigenous beliefs and actions. The exhaustion and danger arising from living within racist societies forms an additional barrier to work/study, and at the same time increases the risk of mental/physical health problems and associated inequalities in diagnosis and treatment. Moreover, #Colonialist and #Orientalist views of science, philosophy,	If you're BIPOC, social media is a good place to connect, find role models, name inequities, support one another over #Microaggressions and #EverydayRacism, and to vent, sympathise and mobilise.Others may find the following conversations and links to associated media helpful to learn, but remember, if you're not BIPOC these are not places for you to insert yourself, dispute, challenge or oppress. This applies across academia (see the #whiteness entry in this table). Black British Academics https://blackbritishacademics.co.uk Dismantling the Masters House #DTMH www.dtmh.ucl.ac.uk UK Association of Black Psychologists https://ukabpsi.co.uk Black PhD Network www.blackphdnetwork.com The University of Colour https://universityofcolour.com Te Kupenga o MAI Māori and Indigenous Scholar Network www.mai.ac.nz Advisory Council for the Education of Romany and Other Travellers https://acert.org.uk

Chapter 6

B

Problem	Try
social sciences and medicine mean key skills and ways of understanding and expertise are ignored or appropriated, or the ways in which Black, Indigenous and People of Colour might contribute or be cared for are restricted or rejected.	#WhyIsMyCurriculumWhite #WOCinSTEM #BLACKandSTEM #CiteBlackWomen #STEMDiversity #BlackProfessor #BlackLivesMatter #BlackInAcademia #LatinxProfessor #Aboriginal #Torresstrait #FirstNations #BlkWomenSyllabus #MātaurangaMāori #IndigenousKnowledge #DecolonisingKnowledge #Blackintheivory
#Breastfeeding You may need space to feed your infant or express/store milk. You may enjoy feeding but discover you're prevented from doing so in academic spaces (ironically conferences, even ones aimed at #womenshealth are major gatekeepers), which can be frustrating or distressing. Alternatively, you may already find breastfeeding/expressing exhausting or difficult, especially if your baby is sick or disabled. Trans and non-binary people may struggle with support on #milksupply or #chestfeeding.	You can request a quiet place to feed or express and time out to do so, plus a fridge to store milk and facilities for cleaning bottles and making formula. Equally, if you wish to feed in class, at a conference or in another public place you should be able to do that without judgement or without being asked to move or cover up. If you're struggling with feeding/expressing you can get support from breastfeeding cafes and advocates. Breastfeeding Network www.breastfeedingnetwork.org.uk #FedIsBest https://fedisbest.org

Chapter 4

B

Problem	Try
Whether you're feeding a baby or toddler, by breast or bottle, there should be no comments on your choices or #bressure to feed in ways that aren't possible or that make you uncomfortable. #breastfeeding #breastmilk #postpartum #nursing #lactation #pumping #bottlefeeding	La Leche League have information for trans and non-binary parents: www.laleche.org.uk/support-transgender-non-binary-parents And for breastfeeding an adopted baby: www.llli.org/breastfeeding-info/adoption
#Bullying and #Harassment Name calling, restricting opportunities, stealing work, receiving threats, and many other issues, as listed in Chapter 3 (*Be an active bystander*), are sadly commonplace in academia. Although these issues are now more widely reported, this problem does appear to be increasing. The everyday pressures of academia are partly responsible, as are wider societal changes encouraging ableism, racism, LGBTQ+ phobia and sexism. The impact of these on mental and physical health, confidence and everyday life cannot be underestimated.	Chapter 3 describes many areas of bullying and ways to resist, while Chapter 4 sets out what should be provided within academia to reduce and tackle bullying. *The Research Companion: A Practical Guide For the Social Sciences, Health and Development* (Boynton 2016) specifically covers bullying, abuse and harassment (on and offline). For more information and support http://theresearchcompanion.com/bullying

Chapter 1

(Continued)

C

Problem	Try
#CareLeavers Many care leavers (people leaving foster care, residential care or who have otherwise grown up from their immediate or extended family) don't go to university, and may struggle with finding out how to apply, having the confidence to put in an application, or managing while at university if there's no family support. This may extend to not knowing how university works, dealing with poverty, or coping with issues arising from past neglect, trauma, abuse or attachment.	There are more resources in Chapter 2 plus a guide on getting to college here: www.careleavers. com/what-we-do/young-peoples-project/acessingeducation-2 Remember to let supervisors, tutors or colleagues know if you are struggling or need more information about navigating academia. The Leap http://www.unite-group. co.uk/campaign/the-leap
#Carers Looking after partners, relatives or children with disabilities; chronic, degenerative or life-limiting illnesses; or mental health problems can be something we want to do, feel obliged to undertake, or have no choice over. Offering care	Academia should make allowances for carers, including hospital or other health/social care visits, reduced hours, home working and time off for personal respite. However, this may not happen or accommodations may still not be adequate to help. If this is the case, try: Carers Trust https://carers.org

Chapters 2 and 6

Chapter 4

c

Problem	Try
can be made more complicated if we arestruggling with exhaustion, anxiety, sleep deprivation, our own mental or physical health, everyday prejudice and barriers, and work/study stress and obstruction.	International Alliance of Carer Organisations https://internationalcarers.org #caregiver #youngcarer #advocate
#ChronicIllness Living with chronic illness can also mean living with pain, exhaustion, overlapping mental and physical health issues, mobility problems and unpredictability (as you may feel better or worse on particular days without an obvious explanation as to why this may be). A lack of awareness or unrealistic expectations from others may leave you feeling judged, shamed or excluded from events (e.g. because dietary needs, physical access, comfort, energy levels etc are not accounted for). Internalised negative ideas about illness (see *Ableism* entry) may make it harder to seek help, or leave you sad, frustrated and angry.	Curable Health App (for chronic pain) www.curablehealth.com Chronically Academic https://chronicallyacademic.org PainUK https://painuk.org Rare Disease UK www.raredisease.org.uk #spoonie #fatigue #ChronicIllness #InvisibleIllness #ChronicPain #InclusionMatters #ButYouDontLookSick

Chapters 4, 6 and 7

(Continued)

C

Problem	Try
Come down Nobody tells us when you manage to finish a module, land a job, publish, defend your thesis or come home from a conference that you may well feel deflated, anxious, uncertain or demoralised afterwards (see *Doctoral students* entry below). #PhDComedown	If you are able to anticipate this, or tell other people to, it won't necessarily stop the feelings but may help you prepare for them. That may include building in treats over time, creating ways to celebrate and praise yourself, allowing time to relax and recover, and paying attention to what you may feel down about as it might indicate other areas of your life that need attention. Chapter 7 Chapter 6
Chapter 1 *#Competition* Academia has become increasingly competitive so you may feel driven to overwork, compare yourself with others, buy into ratings and rankings (see *Assessment* entry above), or believe you are not good enough or don't measure up (see *Imposter syndrome* entry below).	Because competition is so ingrained it is very difficult to resist. Talking to others can identify where competitive environments are causing harm. Try creating your own progress rewards and celebrate achievements that aren't workplace targets. Put other people's celebrations into context – yes, they may be sharing their latest prize on Instagram but you didn't see them crying in their room last night because they're exhausted, overworked or missing their family. Chapters 2–4 and 6 Chapter 7

C

Problem	Try
#Conferences Conferences are a great way to meet people, share ideas and learn – particularly if you are isolated, have poor supervision or lack institutional support. However, they are frequently not safe, accessible or welcoming. Research conferences beforehand to identify what to expect (including if any bursaries are available): https://theresearchcompanion.com/a-rough-guide-to-conferences If you want to present, research what to do to get your work accepted: https://theresearchcompanion.com/how-to-choose-a-conference-then-write-an-abstract-that-gets-you-noticed	Use the ideas in Chapter 4 to prepare a list to find out about and request accommodations and support. Go with friends and support colleagues. Follow remotely on live broadcasts, or using hashtags or skype. Let others know you will be attending and share a photo of what you look like so they can find you. Get training in presentation skills, posters, networking, chairing and timekeeping (see below). Ask for any conference guidelines and ground rules, and ensure you have a clear timetable, travel/accommodation details and maps (see Boynton 2016, pp. 217–272). If you're asked to speak at a conference or other event, make your attendance dependant on there being a range of under-represented minorities also there presenting, and prepare to step aside to allow others with less privilege but the same, or greater, skills than you a platform. Use the same approach if you are planning any inclusive activities.

Chapter 4

(Continued)

C

Problem	Try
#*Contraception and* #*sexualhealth* I've had numerous conversations with students and staff about contraception choices, problems with accessing contraception, side effects of using contraception, fertility worries (see *Fertility* entry), pregnancy planning (see *Pregnancy* entry), using contraception to help with heavy or irregular periods (see *Menstruation* entry), #safersex and #STIs. Plus, accessing contraception while away studying/ working, whether it's safe to travel with contraceptives (particularly condoms) and what to do if you've had unprotected sex.	Find out about different types of contraception here: www.contraceptionchoices.org (Access to some of these may be affected by location/budget.) Your doctor, nurse or contraception/ reproductive health clinic can discuss options that suit your needs and circumstances, including the possibility of #LARC (long-acting reversible contraception) for women doing fieldwork etc). Other specialist services may be available for #LGBTQ+, young people and #sexworkers. NHS Live Well www.nhs.uk/live-well/sexual-health Terrence Higgins Trust guides to #HIV and sexual health www.tht.org.uk/hiv-and-sexual-health Prepster https://prepster.info

Chapter 2

Chapters 3 and 4

D

Problem	Try
#Data We might struggle with data analysis, data management tools and organising data (keeping it entered, clean and up to date, and avoiding losing it – see *Backups* entry).	Use any training available in your place of work/study or available externally (books, websites, online tutorials). Schedule plenty of time to enter, clean, analyse and organise data, especially if a busy period is anticipated. If it starts to become overwhelming reflect on why this may be, if you need additional support, or cut back or change your working practices. Links to software to support researchers can be found here: https://theresearchcompanion. com/chapterlinks How to #cleanyourdata https://theresearchcompanion. com/cleandata Chapter 7
#Deadlines	See *Time* entry (p. 181) and scheduling tips in Chapter 7.
#Disability	See *Ableism* entry.
Disciplinary/dismissal These procedures need clearly outlining and executing fairly, as do instructions on what may be constituted as misconduct for students and staff, appeals procedures and the right to union/legal support. Organisational manuals and regulations ought to cover this but often do	Going through any kind of disciplinary meeting can feel stressful whatever the outcome. Using your support network, particularly your union, identifying what should be provided by your place of work/study (and what isn't), plus collating evidence and getting witnesses is important, as may be calming skills. Citizens Chapter 2 Chapter 4 Chapter 3 Chapter 7

(Continued)

D

Problem	Try
Chapter 4 not (see *The Three Os* entry).	Advice www.citizensadvice.org.uk/ work/leaving-a-job/dismissal/ check-if-your-dismissal-is-fair
Chapter 1, pp. 16–17 Chapter 5 Chapter 1 *#DoctoralStudents* Studying for a #PhD is a unique experience that brings with it all kinds of opportunities. However, it may also be a source of stress if you are experiencing supervisor problems, can't decide what to study, if your research goes wrong, if you don't feel confident, when you're a minority scholar, or when there are other life events affecting you. It's normal to find undertaking a PhD challenging, but nevertheless getting advice and networking with other postgraduates can help (see also *Finance* and *Teaching skills* entries).	Chapter 2 Chapter 3 Chapter 7 Most doctoral students agree having support, seeking help and self-care is vital. You can also try: *The Routledge Doctoral Student's Companion*. Pat Thompson (2010), Routledge. *Before The Dissertation: A Textual Mentor for Doctoral Students at Early Stages of a Research Project*. Christine Pearson Casanave (2014), University of Michigan Press. Helen Kara's books for students cover all areas of the PhD process: https://helenkara.com/writing/ know-more-publishing The Professor is In http://theprofessorisin.com ThinkWell www.ithinkwell.com.au Thrive PhD www.thrive-phd.com PhD Balance https://phdbalance.com The Thesis Whisperer https://thesiswhisperer.com #Thesis #PhDChat #PhDHelp #Dissertation #PhDAdvice #WriteThatPhD #PhDForum #PhDLife #PhDBalance #PhDParenting #AcademicChatter #PostgraduateLife #PhDTopTips

E

Problem	Try
#*Email* You may feel like you're swamped by emails, can't keep up with correspondence or are pressured to respond to everything you're sent, particularly if your organisation has unrealistic targets (e.g. you have to reply to all messages within 24 hours; see *Assessment* entry).	Clean email folders and delete emails regularly. Use clear email titles and folders to find messages. Tag urgent/need to reply messages with a star/mark. Set a specific, scheduled time to check and answer emails. Only answer things that require a reply. Put FAQs or key information online or in a booklet/syllabus linked in your signature, or use generic replies. Use email apps/ management software. Set up out of office (OOO) replies. Take your email off your phone. Unless necessary, reply as briefly as possible. Remember data protection, confidentiality and professionalism in any emails you send, and save and report any abusive emails you receive. #InboxZero #EmailTips

(Continued)

E

Problem	Try
#Essays Learning to write essays is a key skill many of us struggle with, not least if we don't have clear instructions on how to do it or feedback on how to improve. Managing our time, searching literature, refining and submitting on time are all challenging. It's also an effort to produce essay titles, to teach classes that will inform those *#assignments*, and then to mark essays and handle any questions or complaints arising once grades are received. You may be under considerable pressure to get grades and may be tempted to use essay mills or plagiarise, but be aware this may result in you failing a particular essay or module, or facing wider disciplinary procedures within your place of study.	Accept any training in essay writing skills that may be available from your tutor, library or student support services, or from online guides (see also Boynton 2016, pp. 33 and 38). Remember, if you are unhappy about your grade follow-up on feedback, check if you have covered what was required, look at other example essays, attend additional support sessions and ask your tutor how to improve. Being honest about how much effort you made is good. Remember, many papers are double marked to a rubric so requests for a regrade may not be met. If they are, your grade may well stay the same, go up or go down. For lecturers, having time to prepare and grade is important, as is challenging tight turnaround times or ridiculous volumes of essays to mark. Teacher training can help, as can your union and getting feedback from colleagues on what are reasonable and unacceptable demands (see *Teaching skills* entry).

Chapters 2 and 4

E

Problem	Try
#*Exams* Many of the issues described above about essays also apply to exams. They can be your chance to show off all you know, but can also be stressful if you are not confident in a subject or haven't revised. In some cases, you may know the subject but other issues, such as anxiety, get in the way. Chapter 6 Setting exams, invigilating and marking are all skills that need learning. You should expect induction and instructions, feedback, and the opportunity to practice or ask questions, particularly if you are working around specific regulations about accessibility, double marking or special considerations. If this isn't provided by your work request it, and also check Chapter 4 what more experienced colleagues can advise.	Remember to ask for reasonable adjustments if you need more time, a scribe or reader, buff coloured exam papers or other aids to complete your work. If there are extenuating circumstances or special considerations these also need recording as soon as you are able. It is much more difficult to account for problems, sickness or other issues if tutors hear of them once your work has been submitted and graded. 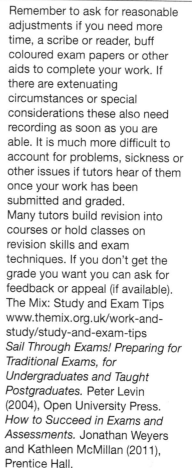 Chapter 4 Many tutors build revision into courses or hold classes on revision skills and exam techniques. If you don't get the grade you want you can ask for feedback or appeal (if available). The Mix: Study and Exam Tips www.themix.org.uk/work-and-study/study-and-exam-tips *Sail Through Exams! Preparing for Traditional Exams, for Undergraduates and Taught Postgraduates.* Peter Levin (2004), Open University Press. *How to Succeed in Exams and Assessments.* Jonathan Weyers and Kathleen McMillan (2011), Prentice Hall.

(Continued)

F

Problem	Try
#Failure Lots of things don't work the first time – or at all. Yet academia implies anything other than brilliance is a problem. Chapter 1 If you're from a minority group you may also have internalised messages that leave you feeling inadequate, or you may fail due to policies and prejudices outside your control. Mental health problems often leave us blaming or shaming ourselves for things that aren't our fault, or cause us to view everything as hopeless or a failure. Chapter 6	#ReclaimingFailure is a really good way to resist messages of competitiveness and idealism. Make space to #makemistakes, ask #questions, raise uncertainties, or have multiple chances to #rework and #revise ideas. If you search online using the phrase 'A CV of Failures' you'll find other people sharing all the things that didn't go so well for them. Remember, many successful people in all fields faced barriers, got things wrong or missed out on opportunities before making things work. It is fine to say something isn't working for you and leave it behind – you haven't failed, you let it go. Chapter 8 *The Examined Life: How We Lose and Find Ourselves.* Stephen Grosz (2014), Vintage. *The Importance of Disappointment.* Ian Craib (1994), Routledge. How To Fail – with Elizabeth Day podcast https://howtofail.podbean.com #SecondChance #StartOver #WeGoAgain #LetItGo
#Family problems	See Chapter 2.

F

Problem	Try
#Fertility You may be #childfree by choice or unsure whether to start a family. Alternatively, you might be struggling after babyloss (see *Babyloss* entry) or with fertility problems. You may be unsure whether to continue a pregnancy or can't agree with a partner what to do, or you may know you need a #termination. You may have concerns about looking for work or continuing with your studies while trying to conceive (#TTC) or while pregnant. Nobody can decide for you whether you should continue with a pregnancy or TTC, but you can discuss options with your support network.	You can get advice on fertility questions from your doctor or this guide from the NHS: www.nhs.uk/conditions/infertility If you want a termination you can organise this via your GP and BPAS (UK): www.bpas.org Or Find A Provider (for the US, Canada, Mexico and more): https://prochoice.org/think-youre-pregnant/find-a-provider If you're childfree but not by choice there's help via Gateway Women: https://gateway-women.com The Uterus Monologues https://uterusmonologues.com Uber Barrens Club https://uberbarrens.club
#Finance This may include worries about your #income, #poverty and #debt; questions about how to fund your studies; or concerns over the pressure to 'bring in money', not knowing where to find funding, and the endless cycle of applying for funding and being rejected (see later in this chapter).	You may find courses and materials on finance and fundraising within your organisation, or at events organised through conferences or professional networks, including funding bodies (see also *Poverty* entry below). Personal Finance for PhDs http://pfforphds.com The Frugal PhD https://www.frugalphd.com

Chapter 2

Chapter 6

(Continued)

F

Problem	Try
#FirstGeneration You might be the first of your family to get a job in academia and/or go to college. This may be a huge source of pride for you, and for your family. Simultaneously you may experience a number of difficulties such as not knowing how academia works, being unsure about #studyskills or #classroometiquette, being treated as an #outsider because of your accent, or other prejudices linked to race, class, disability or sexuality. You may find your values and experiences are not welcomed in academia, despite having much to offer, or that tensions may arise if you feel you neither fit in at home or in academia. Take time to acknowledge and celebrate this is new to you and that is okay.	Holding onto what you've achieved is important, as is allowing yourself not to know everything and recognising other students/staff may be doing better not because they are smarter, but because they grew up knowing the system and benefiting from privileges you haven't had. Find out as much as you can about where you'll be working/studying via their website, open days, by talking to existing staff/students, and reading guides online about what to expect as a student, researcher, lecturer etc. If there are any classes offered about study skills, how to use the library or other inductions, take them. You can also check online for vlogs and podcasts or broaden your support network to include both #FirstGen scholars and others who may have more experience to share. Chapter 2 First in the Family www.firstinthefamily.org *Moving Up Without Losing Your Way: The Ethical Costs of Upward Mobility.* Jennifer M. Morton (2019), Princeton University Press. *Expectations for Classroom Presences.* Rhonda Ragsdale http://funknbeans.com/2013/02/why-is-my-prof-annoyed-with-me-expectations-for-classroom-presence
#Friendships	See Chapter 2.

G

Problem	Try
#Graduation You've worked for years on your degree, perhaps spent your earnings/savings on it and maybe had help from your family. You'll have made sacrifices and learnt a lot. It's a key life event, yet some people struggle with graduation because of the cost of hiring gowns or other expenses; accessibility (either for them or their guests); having struggled with studies or had them blighted by prejudice, abuse or falling out with friends; or not getting the degree they wanted. Anxiety conditions or being neurodiverse may also make the experience feel threatening or overwhelming.	You don't have to go to graduation if you don't want to. You can celebrate in other ways with people you choose, and in a place that's special and affordable. Using second-hand or borrowed clothes, assistance to hire gowns and getting friends and family to take photographs can cut costs. If you are liable to be anxious or feel panicked you can find out what to expect via your college website, watch past videos online of ceremonies, ask for extra assistance from tutors and the graduate office, speak to your doctor about any temporary medical treatments to try and practice relaxation techniques. Remember to ask about accessibility to make sure you can be part of all aspects of your graduation ceremony.

Chapter 6

Chapter 7

Chapter 4

#graduating
#GraduationDay
#GraduationTime
#GraduationCeremony
#GraduationPower
#degree #diploma
#GraduationStudent
#ClassOf #JustGraduated
#alumnus
#GuessWhoGraduated

(Continued)

G

Problem	Try
#Grief and #bereavement Losing a loved one is always difficult (see *Babyloss* entry), however it happened. You may also find yourself grieving for relationships that have ended; over friends, students or workmates you have had to say goodbye to; or letting a job, course or project go.	You should be entitled to time off to visit loved ones if you know they are at the end of their life (see also *Carers* entry), to attend funerals or have compassionate leave after a death.

Chapter 8

Chapter 4

Allowing yourself to grieve and noting bereavement is unpredictable and challenging, rather than assuming there'll be a steady, upward road to recovery is important. You may experience mental or physical health difficulties following a bereavement, or struggle emotionally for many months or even years afterwards. You won't ever 'get better' or 'back to normal'. Instead, you'll adjust to your new situation, finding ways to remember the person or people you've lost. Not everyone needs counseling after loss, but you may find it helpful if you are struggling or if the bereavement was particularly traumatic. This may include supporting students/staff after the death of a friend or colleague.
Refuge in Grief
www.refugeingrief.com

Chapter 6

Chapter 1,
pp. 25–29

#GriefSupport #GriefJourney #grieving #GriefAndLoss #LifeAfterLoss #death #GriefAwareness #GriefQuotes #funeral #mourning

H

Problem	Try	
#Holidays You may struggle with holidays because of finances or being unable to take breaks. You may have no home to go to over the holidays because of estrangement, violence, visa problems or refugee status. While many of us appreciate time off, particularly longer winter and summer breaks, for those of us who crave routine (especially if you are neurodiverse or anxious), a lot of unstructured time can be overwhelming.	If you're unable to take all the holidays you're entitled to, use professional organisations and unions to establish your rights. If you are able to get a break from work/study but not relief from other responsibilities, you might use different parts of your support network, charities or paid assistance for respite. If you are anxious about a lack of routine then create structure by scheduling revision, work, catching up on outstanding tasks, time to relax, volunteering, reading etc over the course of a break. While designed as a virtual home for the winter holidays for LGBTQ+ youth, Your Holiday Mom may be comforting for anyone, during any holiday, if you feel alone: http://yourholidaymom.com	 Chapter 4 Chapter 7, pp. 216–219
#Homesickness Leaving our friends or family to study or work may either be a temporary or longer-term change, which will potentially be affected by budget, visas, conflict or time. You can feel	Feel connected with email, skype, sharing photos, talking on the phone, creating WhatsApp groups or sending letters. Finding people on or offline that share your culture, sense of humour and speak your language can be comforting. Campus societies can create a	

(Continued)

H

Problem	Try
homesick if you are apart from your loved ones/ community for just a matter of days, and certainly if apart for longer. You may also feel like this whether 'home' is an hours travel away, the other side of the world or in several places.	home away from home, including cooking together and sharing news. Podcasts or online radio stations broadcasting in your language can also be comforting. Find the sound of home with Radio Garden: http://radio.garden.

Chapter 2

Homophobia (LGBTQ+ phobia) While staff and students in some countries may be able to be out and proud, in other countries the law makes it exceptionally dangerous to be LGBTQ+. While some institutions may have LGBTQ+ clubs and societies, rights and respect are not necessarily afforded by other staff or students. Fieldwork, travel, attending conferences, training, teaching and everyday life may be dangerous for LGBTQ+ individuals. The mental health of LGBTQ+ people (particularly trans, non-binary and bi folk) is often poor (see links opposite), and while the LGBTQ+ umbrella should welcome all, tensions within the community are painful and difficult to	We've much to celebrate and be proud of in the LGBTQ+ community (including me, a bi woman). We can be role models, enjoy Pride celebrations, honour our elders and mentor youth. Not everyone feels safe to be out – and that is their choice. Never out someone you believe to be LGBTQ+, particularly in locations where being LGBTQ+ is repressed or punished by imprisonment or death. GLAAD www.glaad.org The Bisexual Index www.bisexualindex.org.uk Student Minds www.studentminds.org.uk/ lgbtq.html Switchboard https://switchboard.lgbt YMSM LGBT www.ymsmlgbt.org Stonewall www.stonewall.org.uk Mind LGBTIQ+ mental health www.mind.org.uk/information-support/guides-to-support-and-services/lgbtiqplus-mental-health

H

Problem	Try
cope with, particularly around trans rights, bi erasure and lesbian visibility. Intersections with sexuality, poverty, race and disability frequently mean minorities are disadvantaged or face prejudices from other privileged LGBTQ+ people, or straight people in their communities.	Black Rainbow www.blackrainbow.org.au UK Black Pride https://www.ukblackpride.org.uk Global Sexual Orientation Laws https://ilga.org/ maps-sexual-orientation-laws #Homophobia #Biphobia #Lesbophobia #Transphobia #GayPride #BiPride #LesbianPride #TransPride #LWithTheT #RainbowRevolution #Queer #QueerSTEM #NonBinary #TwoSpirit
#Housework #Cleaning distracts me from frustrations and worries. At this current moment my house is in disarray because of this book, but once it's done I'll have a marathon tidy. You can disagree, we all have different preferences. I love cleaning but hate ironing, which you might like. Although any household chore may be annoying, irrelevant or exhausting if you are struggling with being overworked, relationship or gender inequalities, health difficulties, disabilities or other commitments.	Identify what chores may be needed: vacuuming, sweeping or mopping floors; wiping down surfaces; dusting; tidying away; mending, sorting and cleaning laundry, ironing and putting clothes away; washing windows; cleaning bathrooms and kitchens; making beds; making shopping lists, doing the shopping and putting it away; preparing and cooking meals; washing up; gardening and mowing. Break these down then identify what needs doing daily, weekly, monthly or less frequently and draw up a schedule search online for 'creating a cleaning schedule' for downloadable charts).

Chapter 7,
pp. 216–221

H

Problem	Try
	There may be jobs you love doing that your housemates/children/partner/relatives hate, so you can swap. Note also that if there are things you dislike you may believe you spend a lot longer on them, which can skew your perceptions of how much effort you are making. This, in turn, may put unfair emotional or physical labour onto others. Try a rota. Are there any tasks you can pay someone else to do (e.g. a cleaner), make easier (e.g. online shopping) or do less frequently? This may be helpful if you live alone and feel overwhelmed by having to do everything yourself. Katie Berry's *Cleaning On Your Schedule: Discovering the Cleaning Routine That Works For You.* (2016), Create Space Independent Publishing. Clean your workspace https://theresearchcompanion.com/tidyup The January Cure, Apartment Therapy www.apartmenttherapy.com/collection/the-january-cure Marie Kondo www.apartmenttherapy.com/collection/the-january-cure Unpaid Work Calculator www.ons.gov.uk/visualisations/dvc376/index.html

H

Problem	Try
	#housework #cleaning #laundry #housekeeping #cleaninghacks #cleanwithme #cleaningmotivation #cleaningtips #homemanagement
#Housing Whether it's a room in a shared house or hotel, temporary #accommodation, flat, house, #fraternity or #sorority house, or halls of residence you should feel safe and comfortable. Unfortunately issues with rent or mortgage costs, housing discrimination, 'studentification', racism, relocation, neighbourhood disputes, accessibility and finding a home that fits the needs of you, and possibly other dependents, can be stressful.	If you are living on campus there may be residential committees/ associations that deal with any housing/neighbourhood issues and the student union/societies can also help. Cleaners, porters and accommodation officers can address broken, damaged or unsafe living spaces, and security should attend to antisocial behaviour. You can also find house shares or other accommodation advertised on campuses or, if you're in health settings or bigger organisations, on noticeboards or local community social media pages. Any neighbourhood or community problems may be reported to housing officers or police. International Union of Tenants www.iut.nu

(Continued)

I

Problem	Try
#*Imposter syndrome* In 1978 Pauline Rose Clance and Suzanne Imes coined this now famous phrase we hear a lot of in academia. It refers to that familiar feeling many of us have that no matter how hard we've studied or worked, what qualifications, achievements, and experience we have, we still do not belong, aren't really all that clever or talented, and that at any moment our flaws will be exposed. Unsurprisingly it tends to strike when we're thinking of applying for work or study, during interviews, at conferences, or when teaching or learning. Minorities, first generation scholars and those who are mentally or physically unwell are particularly affected.	Your support network can remind you that this may not just be 'all in your head'. Increasingly organisations are offering training events for students/staff to help overcome imposter syndrome, which may be worth attending, but you should be alert to uncritical approaches that focus on picking up your confidence rather than acknowledging and dismantling the systems of oppression that have made academia so difficult for you to access, navigate and thrive within in the first place. Imposter syndrome is often exacerbated by toxic work/study spaces where it isn't a case of people convincing themselves they *don't* belong when they *do*. It's that they *do* belong but they're told they *don't*, and where structures and systems are designed to keep them out. Moreover, BIPOC, LGBTQ+, working class and disabled people may have internalised prejudice that makes them feel they do not deserve to be there, or they may have grown up experiencing abelism, racism and classism that has consistently held them back and shut them out. Valerie Young www.impostersyndrome.com Pauline Rose Clance https://paulineroseclance.com/ impostor_phenomenon.html

Chapter 3

Chapter 1

I

Problem	Try
International students and staff Loneliness, isolation, uncertainty, financial worries, food and dietary issues and racism are all issues faced by international students who may find the customs, culture and communities in which they are living, working or studying to be challenging. This is particularly likely if students/staff are not fully informed prior to travel what their work and living situation will be. Although there are plenty of guides that exist to help with this, most are written in English and focus on students from outside the UK/US studying in those countries.	Having clear information on what to expect from a degree course or job can be helpful in avoiding problems. This might include clear and realistic instructions on the following points: The culture, customs and laws of where you'll be living and working. How things work – even the basics of going to the shop, using public transport or dealing with the weather might be different from home. Visa requirements. How much things cost (including travel, accommodation, medicines and healthcare, food, heating, clothing etc). Where you'll be living and, if based at a university, whether your accommodation is on campus or a distance from it (and how to reach it). Specific information on what will be required from work/study and how academic practices may be significantly different from one institution/country to another (particularly on topics such as plagiarism, exams, classroom etiquette). Information on where to find local communities that share your language or the opportunity to create international student groups.

Chapter 2

(Continued)

I

Problem	Try
	Most universities have a specific office or tutor dedicated to supporting international staff/students. Pre-arrival and orientation information for these individuals about what to bring to college and what to expect once there are available from most university websites. Increasingly students are creating their own information using Instagram, vlogs or Facebook to explain to other international students what to expect in a particular country and/or university, and how to navigate life there. UK Council for International Student Affairs (UKCISA) www.ukcisa.org.uk Erasmus www.erasmusprogramme.com
#Introverts and #shyness Not everyone enjoys busy, noisy social events or work/study spaces. It may be you are shy, introverted, anxious or neurodiverse and so prefer smaller groups or your own company, or that you struggle to understand the complexities of social situations and interpersonal relationships.	Forcing yourself into situations that make you uncomfortable is bad for your mental and physical health. Give yourself permission to enjoy solitary and quiet pursuits. Prepare for situations when you'll be in contact with others so you can relax before and after, and have an exit route planned. Headphones with soft music or white noise can be invaluable if you can't go somewhere to shut off. If you're happy with your own company still let people know where you are to ensure you stay safe.

Chapter 7

Chapter 4

I

Problem	Try	
#Isolation It could be your location, your mental or physical health, disability, language skills, confidence, income or research topic that restricts who you can interact with. You can also feel lonely if you're away from home (see *Homesickness* entry), are doing fieldwork (see *Safety* entry), or if you are a lone worker. Sometimes you can be surrounded by people but still feel lonely or an outsider because of your race, age, disability, gender, sexuality, politics or faith (or any intersections of these).	Widening your support network and socialising on and offline may make you feel more connected, as may scheduling in time to keep in touch with loved ones. You can also look through the links in this chapter to find hashtags and organisations of people like you to check in with, particularly if you are in isolation or mandatorily working from home. Unison (UK Union) has a guide for Lone Working that may be of use if much of your work/study is done alone: www.unison.org.uk/content/uploads/2016/10/Working20alone.pdf	Chapter 2 Chapter 7

(Continued)

J

Problem	Try
Job seeking	Your networks can be invaluable in helping you locate jobs, swerve dodgy departments, and reduce job-seeking doubts and nerves. If you're on campus there may be services to help you pick a career, sort your CV, learn to write cover letters and practice interview techniques. Online courses, films and blogs are also worth searching for general job-seeking tips. Chapter 2

Major stressors people have shared with me include getting qualified; finding a job; preparing a CV and cover letter; getting to interview; performing well at the interview; and being offered a job.
Academia is a hugely competitive and frequently destructive place, meaning even if you have done all the 'right things' to find a job you may be facing hundreds of applications, interviews and rejections. Even the top performing institutions experience redundancies. The idea that polishing your CV, learning interview techniques and having a great cover letter will bring you a good job in a secure department is not true. It's not to say you mustn't try, but it would be remiss of me to suggest it's that easy.

Graduate Recruitment Bureau
www.grb.uk.com/careers-advice
A round up of employer and funding sites
can be found here:
https://theresearchcompanion.com/resources

 Chapter 8

K

Problem	Try	
Keeping up Alongside feeling overwhelmed and overworked you may be struggling to manage information, demands and other pressures. Not only are you supposed to be studying/working, having a social life, attending to your personal life, and keeping fit and healthy, you're also supposed to be documenting everything for social media and sharing your successes, while noting what everyone else is doing and trying to match them (see *Competition* entry).	Assess your schedule and see what you are able to drop or rearrange. Cut things you don't enjoy and that aren't bringing any value. Check where you may be engaged in behaviours that aren't helping your mental or physical health. Take advice from your union or professional organisations if you believe you are being pushed to achieve unreasonable or unattainable goals.	Chapter 7 Chapter 6 Chapters 2 and 4

(Continued)

L

Problem	Try
#Language barriers If you're working in a second or third language; are trying to honour or sustain your indigenous language; lack interpreters (including for sign language and fingerspelling); or are learning a new language alongside your studying/ work, you may feel isolated (see *Isolation* entry), stressed, and struggle to follow instructions or be aware of your rights and responsibilities. This can Chapter 4 put you at risk or affect Chapter 6 your wellbeing.	Your place of work/study may have language courses available or you may pay privately for a course, access one via the community, or through refugee or asylum seeker networks (if appropriate). You may also find local radio, television (particularly soap operas), newspapers or tuning in to everyday conversations around you helps familiarise you with a new language. This may be particularly helpful if you have learned a formal version of a language but are struggling with the faster, colloquial use you're now experiencing, or with the complexities of academic conversations. Alert your supervisor, colleagues or employer if you are struggling, or if those around you are not making an effort to help you communicate. Try not to let embarrassment or shame stop you asking for help Chapter 4 you are entitled to, particularly if it is affecting your ability to work or study. It's okay to let friends or colleagues know you are struggling or ask them to help you understand things, particularly if you are lacking confidence in speaking or writing a language.

L

Problem	Try
	You could offer your skills as a translator, interpreter or language tutor. Chapter 2, pp. 60–61
	If you are working or studying alongside someone who is learning a language, being patient and encouraging is important. A key academic skill is being able to work with different groups, so appreciating how a colleague or course mate may be learning two roles (job/course and language) while you're only doing one could remind you to be more positive. If you are concerned that they aren't coping or are being bullied, let a colleague or tutor know.
#Learningdifficulties and disabilities As noted in Chapter 4, institutions should provide accommodations and support if you need additional assistance to understand instructions, equipment or other activities you are undertaking. Chapter 6 has advice if your #LDs are affecting your mental health. #learningdisabilities #adhd #dyspraxia #dyslexia #dyslexic #dyspraxic #specialneeds #learningdisability #SEND #executivefunctioning	Find out what support is available, and if you can join any support networks or groups for students or staff with #LDs. The Complete University Guide information for dyslexic students www.thecompleteuniversityguide.co.uk/universities/dyslexic-students'-university-guide The Dyslexic Academic https://www.dyslexicacademic.com *Academic Writing and Dyslexia: A Visual Guide to Writing at University.* Adrian J. Wallbank (2018), Routledge.

(Continued)

L

Problem	Try
	Study Skills for Students With Dyslexia. Sandra Hargreaves and Jamie Crabb (2016), Sage. *How to Succeed with Specific Learning Difficulties at College and University: A Guide for Students, Educators and Parents.* Amanda Kirby (2013), Souvenir Press. *The Dyspraxic Learner: Strategies for Success.* Alison Patrick (2015), Jessica Kingsley Publishers. SKILL: National Bureau for Students with Disabilities www.skill.org.uk
#Loneworking Being able to set your own schedule, work by yourself and decide what you're going to do might sound heavenly but can be challenging. You may feel vulnerable, bored or struggle with a lack of structure; or feel overwhelmed with instructions, demands and requests, and feel like you can't keep up, particularly if you've not chosen to be a lone worker.	Being very clear on your own safety (see *Safety* entry) is important, as is using your network. Professional organisations can help you keep up with news, events and opportunities. The tips on motivation (*Motivation entry* below) may keep you going, while using a schedule and having clear boundaries is important. You can still join a union even if you aren't in a university as your rights need protecting wherever you are in academia.

Chapter 7

Chapter 4

M

Problem	Try
#Menopause Because of stigma, sexism and ageism, little attention is given to menopause, in particular in supporting menopausal staff and students. The volume, severity and duration of psychological and physical symptoms, along with the lack of information about what is going on and the treatment options available, may leave women feeling isolated and embarrassed. Black women may experience more symptoms with greater severity, yet receive less information and sub-standard care. Trans men may experience menopausal symptoms as part of their transitioning, which may be unexpected and difficult to manage, as well as potentially #dysphoric.	Support from other people going through menopause from forums, self-help groups and your own network can be reassuring, give you ideas about treatment or self-care and about what to speak to your doctor about. Being able to speak more openly about menopause and having more accommodations made within work around breaks, workload, dealing with #brainfog, #moodchanges, #bleeding, sleep issues, #HotFlushes etc, alongside being able to incorporate those, without awkwardness, into work/study spaces is also important. Menopause Support https://menopausesupport.co.uk International Menopause Society links www.imsociety.org/links.php #MakeMenopauseMatter

Chapter 2

(Continued)

M

Problem	Try
#Menstruation It may be your #periods are problem free, but if they are heavy, irregular or painful (or any combination of these) it may impact negatively on your life. While in some places periods can be discussed openly, in others it remains taboo. Not everyone wants to celebrate their periods, but being able to accommodate them within work/study spaces would be more inclusive for women, non-binary folk and trans men who still menstruate. Not having access to sanitary protection excludes many from education so providing sanitary protection (#SanPro) in bathrooms, departmental offices, staff/student common rooms or unions is something you could organise. Note that #PeriodPoverty rarely exists in isolation so referring people to food banks and other sources of support is also worthwhile.	Try stronger pain relief, hormonal contraception, hot water bottles or heat pads, dietary adjustments and rearranging your schedule if your periods are particularly disruptive. Seek medical advice if you're concerned by erratic, painful or heavy periods (see *Contraception* entry above). The options for managing your period are more varied now (depending on where you are located) and include more environmentally friendly options, such as washable/reusable towels or period pants, which may help if you're in a low income country or doing fieldwork where it's difficult to access disposable sanitary protection. You might consider a long-acting reversible contraceptive (LARC) for the duration of your project (see *Contraception* entry). Pelvic Pain Support Network www.pelvicpain.org.uk/conditions/painful-periods-dysmenorrhoea/ Endometriosis Society www.endometriosis-uk.org *The Vagina Bible: The Vulva and the Vagina. Separating Myth From Medicine.* Jennifer Gunter (2019), Citadel.

Chapter 2

Chapter 2

M

Problem	Try
#Mental health	See Chapters 2 (seeing a doctor); 4 (accommodations); and 6 (symptoms); plus Chapter 7 for self-care ideas.
#Motivation If you don't feel like doing anything it may be a sign you need a break, have too much going on, are really anxious about a looming deadline, or are bored, uninspired or unsupported. Building breaks into your schedule and routines may motivate you, but be alert if you are doing this and still struggling. Sometimes you're not motivated because you're in the wrong job or on the wrong course. Consider whether it's time to move on.	If you know the reason you're not motivated you can work to change that with more training, caring for yourself, or taking on a new or different task to break the monotony. Sometimes even if things are dull you still have to do them. Building in rewards can help. Additional supervision, letting your supervisor/colleagues know you are struggling or taking on training may make things easier. Try also identifying your Golden Time – points in the day when you've more enthusiasm. If you're overwhelmed or struggling to keep up you may want to break down all that's on your plate and prioritise tasks so that you can take one on at a time. You can use your schedule to plan ahead.

(Continued)

M

Problem	Try
	If you're not motivated because you can't cope or aren't interested in what you are doing, try delegating or swapping (ensuring you aren't skipping key things you should be doing or imposing on others). Working collectively can make a boring task more fun and less lonely. Some people like to set 'do not disturb' notices on their office doors or timetables, out of hours message on their emails, or have set work from home or library days where they cannot be interrupted. If you're struggling just to get started or to keep going, try the #Pomodoro Technique: https://francescocirillo.com/pages/pomodoro-technique Or the tips and resources from The Happy Academic: https://happyacademic.wordpress.com The Effective Academic: http://effectiveacademic.ca Or *How to be an Academic Superhero Establishing and Sustaining a Successful Career in the Social Sciences, Arts and Humanities.* Ian Hay (2017), Edward Elgar Publishing.

N

Problem	Try
#Negativity It's hard to keep going or enjoy yourself if you're in a toxic environment or are overly critical about yourself. Equally, it's hard to feel positive if you're living with inequalities, depression, disability and chronic illness, and are in pain or exhausted.	Chapter 6 has more information if you feel your negativity is a symptom of your mental health or a toxic environment is making you unwell. If your place of work/study is overly negative or making you feel bad, checking what would make your life easier, reinforcing your support network and seeking advice from your union or professional organisations is an excellent idea.
#Neoliberalism	See Chapter 1.

(Continued)

O

Problem	Try
The Three O's Academia is infested with these. #Obfuscation – where you can't find guidance, syllabus, instructions, or key resources, tools or equipment. #Obstruction – where you can't progress. And #Opposition – where other people or situations create barriers. You're more likely to encounter the #3OOOs if you're from a minority group or you are working in a toxic environment Chapters 1 and 3 where particular students/ staff are given more opportunities than others.	Checking your rights, taking union or legal advice and using your networks may help you. Be sure to note the context, for example your supervisor would be wrong to hold your work back over professional jealousy, but right to tell you to wait if they feel your work isn't ready for sharing yet. See #JustDoIt in Chapter 7. Chapters 2 and 4

P

Problem	Try
Participants If you work with people in research, outreach, science/public engagement or other activities you may be concerned about making all you do accessible and inviting. Recruiting people to your studies/ events may be stressful; as may be considering issues of payment; considering the safety/wellbeing of all involved, including yours; how you appropriately react to participants needs; and what to do if, at the end of a study/event, you feel either emotionally invested or drained, or participants don't want to let go.	See Boynton 2016, pp. 113–166.
Pay Money is a major issue in academia including: not getting paid when you should; low wages; overly bureaucratic systems to claim wages or carry out short-term or consultancy roles; paying minorities less for the same role others are paid more for; budget cuts; having to pay up front with your own funds for conferences, travel etc and lengthy delays in being refunded; and setting meetings in locations or at times that are expensive or difficult to get to.	Increasingly people are speaking out about how unfair, time consuming and ridiculous these situations are, particularly on social media, and unions are now taking a greater role in challenging unequal and unfair practices. In relationships we know financial control is a sign of abuse. We need to recognise the same behaviours in academia.

Chapters 1 and 4

Chapter 2

P

Problem	Try
This extends to expecting you to work for free – either blatantly saying there is no fee or expecting you to work way more than your contracted hours in unpaid overtime; providing no additional pay for unsocial hours or demanding or difficult roles; offering no funding for necessary travel, accommodation, training or career development.	
#Perfectionism and #procrastination	See Chapter 6.
#PhD	See *Doctoral students* entry.
#Physicalhealth	See Chapter 2 (seeing a doctor); 4 (accommodations); and 6 (symptoms); plus, Chapter 7 for self-care ideas.
#Politics and #prejudice Globally, academics may be familiar with political upheavals that threaten their work and wellbeing, while marginalised academics worldwide struggle with the impact of #whitesupremacy, colonialism, LGBTQ+ phobia and restriction of women's rights. A few examples at the time of writing include Hungary ending Gender Studies programmes;	While some #AtRiskAcademics hide their sexuality, gender, political views or particular subject interests this isn't always possible or desirable. The following organisations are designed to give specialist advice on keeping safe and seeking asylum. Council for At Risk Academics (CARA) www.cara.ngo Chapters 3 and 4

P

Problem	Try
Brazil, India and Egypt targeting dissenting staff and students with the military on campus and confiscating teaching materials; China and Sudan limiting internet and social media access, restricting visa access and preventing archives being used; neo-Nazis in the US marching on campuses, with white supremacist movements targeting minority scholars; in the UK, Brexit continues to be divisive and disruptive; and finally, LGBTQ+ scholars in Iran, Chechnya and Nigeria have been arrested, tortured and killed. Additionally, wars, political unrest or recessions have also led to academics migrating or seeking asylum. While a global pandemic has caused death, sickness and disruption.	#ScholarsAtRisk, including their 2019 global report 'Freedom to Think' www.scholarsatrisk.org/ resources/free-to-think-2019 #AcademicFreedom #RefugeeAcademics
#Poverty It may be hard to believe in the 21st century that staff and students in academia are reliant on charity or food banks; can't access or afford healthcare; are struggling financially; are permanently or temporarily homeless; have debts and long-term unemployment; or pay that is inadequate to support them or any dependents. Policies of austerity,	Professional organisations, unions and other agencies described in Chapter 2 may be able to provide financial advice or direction to hardship funds, as may charities or Chaplaincy. Food banks, soup kitchens or charity shops are a source of food/ clothing, while housing trusts and homelessness charities can provide advice (including to those who're living in temporary accommodation).

(Continued)

P

Problem	Try
benefit cuts, private healthcare, zero hours contracts and workplace insecurity, however, have impacted on life outside academia as well as within it.	If poverty is impacting on your life (see Chapter 6) your supervisor may be able to advise (see *Finance* entry). Chapter 6
#Precarity	See Chapter 1.
#Pregnancy Being pregnant in academia should be a positive and supportive time whether your pregnancy is straightforward or complex, and regardless of if it goes to term or not. You should get time off for appointments; maternity (and other parental) leave; reasonable adjustments and altered working conditions (e.g. not handling particular dangerous substances, reduced working hours); maternity pay and other benefits. Support should also be available for those that lose a pregnancy (see *Babyloss* entry), or experience additional health problems during or after pregnancy (#birthtrauma or #birthinjury). Where there is sexism, bullying, precarity or competition it may not feel safe nor possible to request the above or reveal a pregnancy until unavoidable. The stress of work/study may also make it difficult to enjoy the pregnancy or attend to any pregnancy worries or problems.	See *Contraception* and *Babyloss* entries, plus Chapter 4 on rights. If your partner is negative, unsupportive or absent, or if you feel unconnected to the pregnancy or experience mental distress you may need additional support from the organisations listed in Chapter 6. Pregnancy Sickness Support www.pregnancysickness support.org.uk Black Mamas Matter Alliance https://blackmamasmatter.org Tommy's Guide to Pregnancy www.tommys.org/pregnancy PANDAS (Pre and postnatal depression) www.pandas foundation.org.uk What to Expect www.whattoexpect.com Birth Trauma Association www.birthtrauma association.org.uk

P

Problem	Try
	LGBT Paths to Parenthood www.nhs.uk/live-well/ healthy-body/ gay-health-having-children
Presenting It might be a job application, union rally address, conference keynote, lecture or public talk – and you may be thrilled to be sharing your ideas or anxious about your skills or abilities to do so.	Your college/workplace may offer training in presenting talks, lectures, posters, videos, podcasts, seminars etc and there are numerous guides for this to be found online. Increasingly as people livestream events or share their presentations afterwards you can observe examples of good practice. There's a whole genre of presentation skills resources out there (see Boynton 2016, pp. 217–272). Echo Rivera's Creative Research Communications www.echorivera.com
	#Conferences #Posters #Powerpoints #Talks #Public Speaking #PublicEngagement #SciComm

Chapter 1, pp. 16–17

(Continued)

P

Problem	Try
#Promotion In an ideal world you work hard, show willing, build your skillset and get promoted. Unfortunately, for most of us that's not how it goes. Promotion happens through a combination of luck, privilege and notoriety (see *Job seeking* entry). Note in some workplaces if you apply internally for promotion you may have to wait a period of time before you can do so again, but you can always seek promotion by applying for a job in another institution.	My cynicism doesn't mean you shouldn't seek promotion, particularly if your skills suggest you qualify. You may do this by looking for job opportunities within your department; checking promotions procedures (which will tell you what you need to move up a grade/role); and asking other people to see their applications. Undertake additional tasks to enhance your skills, including professional certification, obtaining funding, supervising/mentoring staff, outreach/engagement, serving on committees or as a representative. These can be enjoyable to do but can also take up a huge amount of time and energy (often unpaid, see above), so be selective about what you spend your time on. It may help to set yourself a time in which you plan to apply, scheduling in additional activities, training, updating your CV or other things that will benefit you regardless of whether you're promoted or not.

Chapter 8

Chapter 8

P

Problem	Try
	The Essential Guide to Moving Up The Academic Career Ladder. Jobs.ac.uk www.jobs.ac.uk/media/pdf/careers/resources/the-essential-guide-to-moving-up-the-academic-career-ladder.pdf See also the resources in the *Motivation* entry and Academic Positions https://academicpositions.com
#*Publishing* There's a variety of ways you can share your ideas – blogging, reports, books, papers in peer reviewed journals, commentaries, the list goes on (see Chapter 8 in Boynton 2016, pp. 217–272, for a variety of ways to showcase your work). Your discipline will value particular formats (e.g. books and monographs in the humanities, less so in healthcare). If you want to publish in different formats be strategic. Publish as required for your career development while finding other outlets for additional creative urges.	Many institutions and professional bodies offer guides on how to get published, and many journals have guidance (including podcasts and videos) on publication skills (see above). Some conferences for ECRs also offer workshops on getting started/publication advice (including handling rejection). Remember, the feedback you get should be prompt, clear and constructive. You can use or challenge it as appropriate. It should not be belittling, insulting or so brief you can't make sense of it.

(Continued)

P

Problem	Try
The pressure to publish – not just in volume but location and reputation – can be overwhelming, as may the anxiety created when others around you seem to be managing; or the frustration and despair that may come from the endless rounds of submitting papers, rejection or lengthy editing processes and delays from submission to publication. You might also be unsure how to spot a predatory journal or know if you've been taken advantage by one.	You can improve the process of review by volunteering to be a reviewer or on an editorial board, noting that these roles, while counting towards promotion, are rarely paid. Pat Thomson's Patter has lots of writing and publishing advice: https://patthomson.net Think, Check, Submit helps you identify predatory publishers: https://thinkchecksubmit.org Use your networks to get feedback, have help with drafts or revisions, and set up writing clubs on or offline to get motivated. While building in self-care in cases of rejection or celebrating when your work is accepted.
#AcWri #ShutUpAndWrite #AmWriting #AmReading #AmEditing #ReviewerTwo #GetYourManuscriptOut	

Chapter 7

R

Problem	Try
#Rejection Rejection sucks. Whether it's missing out, #dismissal, seeing someone get something you wanted, losing a relationship or your job, or having your visa or work declined. But academia loves it! It runs on rejection, which you're supposed to wear as a badge of honour (along with overwork and not admitting problems). We buy in to being made miserable as a rite of passage, leaving us little space for sadness, frustration, fear or despair.	See resources and ideas in *Failure* entry, plus Boynton 2016, pp. 266–268.
#Relationships	See Chapter 2.
#ResearchSkills and topics I'm such a methods geek I already wrote a book on getting research done (Boynton 2016), so I won't go into more detail here except to say many topics can be triggering, emotionally draining and exhausting. Research settings in and outside academia can be	If you're undertaking a degree there should be research training components built in, and many institutions offer additional courses on specific methodologies and analysis. Many journals, professional organisations and research funding bodies have written, audio or video guides on

(Continued)

R

Problem	Try
dangerous, and the concurrent pressure of impact, competitiveness and precarity can make learning about and undertaking research very difficult (see *Safety* entry).	the how-tos of research (see *Publishing* entry). You can also find numerous formal and informal methodological interest societies on and offline.
#Resilience If there have been problems in your organisation around stress, bullying, absenteeism etc you may have had an external consultant providing 'resilience training'. This may be a range of talks, role plays, exercises or other reflections designed to help you recover from adversity and feel stronger and more proficient. Lots of people have found this reassuring and useful. Others have struggled to make the ideas work in practice, primarily because the wider structures causing their distress have not changed – they're still overworked, underpaid, in unreasonable work/study conditions and uncertain about the future.	We can #ReclaimResilience by noting the circumstances we cannot change, nor should put up with, then creating spaces for ourselves to prioritise our wellbeing, protect our time and energy, support our colleagues and build our confidence. While being well intentioned, resilience has been weaponised to force people to accept toxic or abusive situations, or hold themselves responsible for something they have not caused and cannot fix.

Chapters 2 and 7

Chapter 1

S

Problem	Try
#Safety Your personal safety may be affected by workplace conditions – bullying and harassment, overwork, unsafe work spaces, or poorly maintained (or no) equipment. In addition, travel; the people you interact with during research, events, outreach or teaching; the subject of your research; and undertaking fieldwork can all raise issues of personal safety, emotional distress and uncertain boundaries. The things we hear and see can have a huge impact. While we are taking the issue of safety more seriously it tends to focus around traditional industrial health and safety models and less on psychological reactions and the needs for supervision, debriefing and, where necessary, therapeutic assistance. Unsupportive environments can result in risk taking, exposure to dangerous situations and people blaming themselves, or being blamed by others, for adverse events that could have been prevented or planned for.	See Boynton 2016, pp. 167–198. Along with links to other resources here: https://theresearchcompanion.com/resources #ResearcherSafety #ResearcherWellbeing #HealthAndSafety

Chapter 3

Chapters 4 and 6

Chapter 4

Chapters 1, 3 and 6

(Continued)

S

Problem	Try
#Sexism Despite efforts to increase the number of women within academia, including more women students onto courses where they've previously been underrepresented; provision of maternity/paternity leave; and women-friendly networking events, problems remain. Minority women (particularly those that are poor or Indigenous/Aboriginal) are often excluded by programmes that interpret 'equality' to mean 'white women'. Activities designed to reduce sexism often ignore intersections of race, sexuality, class and disability and mean middle class, straight, white, able-bodied women are given opportunities denied to others. In addition, the failure to implement programmes that might increase equality, such as paternity leave, allow the issue to remain and permit #EverydaySexism to thrive within academic spaces. And when these issues are challenged women are called oversensitive, unreasonable, demanding or accused of exaggerating.	Collective organising has long been a feature of women's movements and having people to acknowledge what you're experiencing, affirm the impact it's having on you, and stand beside you to challenge it can feel reassuring and empowering. Many workplaces and organisations have women's groups you may wish to join (noting some are more welcoming to trans women, #BIWOC, disabled, neurodiverse, lesbians, bi or queer women than others). *Surviving Sexism in Academia: Strategies for Feminist Leadership.* Kirsti Cole and Holly Hassel (2017), Routledge. Women In Academia Support Network www.wiasn.com Black Sister Network https://blackbritishacademics.co.uk/category/blog/black-sister-network Tenure, She Wrote https://tenureshewrote.wordpress.com #CiteHer #MeToo #MeTooAcademia #MeTooSTEM #WomenEd #WIASN

Chapter 1

S

Problem	Try
#SocialMedia It's such an integral part of our lives we struggle to live without it (although that is often a good idea). Social media can help us organise, mobilise, support each other, know we aren't alone, have fun and build relationships. It can also be overwhelming, intrusive, disruptive and a place where we can be targeted, shamed, abused or threatened. Sometimes this remains online or spills offline. Knowing how to navigate and control social media isn't a routinely taught skill. Having been a late adopter, academia largely now views it as a promotional tool to further impact, with little support for students or staff on maintaining boundaries, staying safe, and acting in professional and responsible ways. When things go wrong it's usually left to individuals to cope with any backlash or protect themselves; and while professional standards and guidelines exist, they may be vague and unworkable.	*Social Media for Academics (2nd Ed).* Mark Carrigan (2019), Sage. Andy Miah's *The A–Z of Social Media* https://andymiah.net/a-to-z-of-social-media You do not have to engage with anyone who is abusive, threatening, harasses you or encourages others to pile on so your replies are overwhelmed. It is fine to mute individuals or conversations; block people; leave your direct messages closed; keep comments on blog posts moderated or closed; set up keyword redirects that send abusive email messages and accounts to spam; and report those who're sending abusive or threatening messages to you or others. Social media has allowed the targeting of BIPOC, disabled, women, LGBTQ+ and other minorities, so offering support to those under attack (without copying them into abuse) and reporting those targeting them is important (see Boynton 2016, pp. 225–228).

Chapter 7

Chapter 7, pp. 222–223

(Continued)

S

Problem	Try
#*Student needs* These may vary from requiring practical information on how to navigate the campus, accommodation concerns, study skills, difficulties with supervisors, wanting to change modules, research topics, or degrees; through to mental and physical health problems, accessibility or trying to study while dealing with everyday prejudice.	Your college should have online resources and on campus courses on literature searching, writing, study skills, revision tips etc. If your college doesn't provide this search online, as many others do. You can speak to your personal tutor, other tutors you get along with, chaplaincy, student welfare, union and societies if you want to feel supported, get specific advice about student life or study, or if you need to report any problems that are liable to interrupt your studies or affect your wellbeing. Chapters 2–4 and 6 Student Beans www.studentbeans.com/uk The Complete University Guide www. thecompleteuniversityguide. co.uk #MyDayInHe #HigherEd #eLearning #EdChat #HigherEducation #CollegeChat
#*Supervision*	See *Doctoral students* and *Teaching skills* entries.

T

Problem	Try
#Targets As mentioned in the *Assessment* entry, targets are an increasing problem in academia. This may be a requirement to clean more offices than your shift permits, too much reading to process in a module, or a huge volume of essays to mark in a matter of days. Conversely, setting *yourself* targets, organising your time and building in rewards when you achieve things is a useful technique to help you focus, stay motivated and get things done.	Chapter 7 has more information on ways to manage your time and set achievable and useful targets for yourself. See also *Find out more* at the end of Chapter 4. If you feel overwhelmed with demands and pressured to do things you could try raising this with your colleagues or supervisor to see if you can reduce or change your work/study patterns. If that doesn't work, speaking to your union may give a better sense of what is acceptable and how you can resist if targets are taking over.
#Teaching skills It's a myth that some people are naturally fantastic #teachers. While some have particular skills that can #inspire, #motivate or #advance students, we all have to learn the craft of teaching – which isn't just about good communication, it's about #psychology, #pedagogy and #practice.	Your organisation should offer resources, instructions or training in different #TeachingTechniques; explaining how #MarkingSchemes work; approaches to #StudentEngagement and discipline; #NegotiatingSkills; supporting minority students; understanding and implementing reasonable adjustments; managing student demands and challenging situations; #PastoralCare; #SyllabusDesign; setting and marking exams; invigilation; and project/PhD supervision.

Chapters 2–4

Chapter 7

(Continued)

T

Problem	Try
You may enjoy teaching or find it challenging. It may be you're exhausted from a high teaching load, perhaps coupled with the pressure to research and publish. You may have a teaching-only contract or a mix of teaching and other tasks. There may be some subjects, students or academic years that are easier to teach than others. You may decide what you wish to teach or have no control over what subjects you're required to deliver, nor how many courses you cover or students you support.	However, this may not always be available, in which case online courses, vlogs, podcasts, blogs, resources from teaching unions, workshops at conferences, or sharing skills with or asking advice from other colleagues can help fill the gap in what your organisation should be providing. Your union and colleagues may be especially supportive if you need to manage student grievances and complaints; face managerial pressure to provide teaching, feedback or tutor time you are unable to offer; or report abusive or threatening students. Colleagues, chaplaincy and welfare/counseling (if available) may be able to assist if you are supporting vulnerable students or after a student death (see *Bereavement* entry). *The Lecturers Toolkit: A Practical Guide to Assessment, Learning and Teaching.* Phil Race (2014), Routledge. *An A–Z of Creative Teaching in Higher Education*. Sylvia Ashton and Rachel Stone (2018), Sage. Supervising PhDs https://supervisingphds.wordpress.com

Chapter 4

Chapters 2 and 3

#AcademicTwitter
#AcademicChatter #elearning
#EdChat #EduTwitter #HigherEd
#MedEd

T

Problem	Try
#Technology Our lives have been enriched by technology, allowing us to work more creatively, effectively and remotely; to be able to connect across distance; plus to build, share and invent. For many academics, while technology is an integral and often positive part of their lives, the requirements to learn how to use new systems, databases or devices for teaching, administration and research can feel overwhelming, particularly during emergency situations. As can the volume of emails flooding inboxes every day, or the different accounts you are expected to keep up with. For academics in low income/resource poor countries the ability to get connected, access technology or find academic resources (papers, online courses etc) is greatly reduced.	Having time to learn new technologies, to play and make mistakes is important and should be scheduled into work time. Courses on how to use email effectively (see *Emails* entry), or introductions to other systems can build confidence and save time. If these things aren't available in work you may find online tools and courses useful; but, if you are expected to pay for these or take on new technologies (and pay for gadgets also) this is a matter for Human Resources and, if they aren't reasonable, then your union. Chapters 3 and 4 Author Aid www.authoraid.info/en How to get hold of papers when you don't have access https://theresearchcompanion.com/ how-to-get-hold-of-papers-when-you-dont-have-access

(Continued)

T

Problem	Try
#*Tenure* Competition, precarity and a widening range of academic assessments have made it more difficult for people to obtain tenure in countries/universities where this system exists. This has led to increased stress and overwork, while also leaving those who have not been granted tenure having to work multiple jobs or temporary contracts while waiting (and hoping) to land a tenured position. Minority staff and older people entering the workplace as early career researchers are particularly likely to struggle.	Many universities operating this system have a tenure track path detailing what is required from staff to achieve tenure (and how long they have to do this). It may include detailed, stepwise instructions and the opportunities for mentoring and guidance from a university, equally it may be left to individuals to identify what they'll be assessed on and how to acquire those skills. Informal support systems or professional organisations for early career researchers and PhDs may be particularly helpful in coaching, encouragement and providing examples of successful tenure applications. This may include highlighting what teaching, publishing, funding, and other skills and experiences you'll need to demonstrate, and how to document those. Many of the links to academic-related resources in this chapter, plus Chapters 1 to 3, will also discuss tenure-related issues. Additionally, try:

Chapter 2

T

Problem	Try
	Good Work If You Can Get It: How to Succeed In Academia. Jason Brennan (2020), John Hopkins University Press. *Scaling the Ivory Tower: Your Academic Job Search Workbook.* Hillary Hutchinson and Mary Beth Averill (2019).
	#TenureTrack #adjunct #CareerArc #AdjunctNation #AdjunctLife
#Time We're all under pressure to do too much, to fill our lives and to try and be perfect while working to other people's schedules and wishing there were more hours in the day to be with loved ones or be doing what we love.	Chapter 7 has ideas for managing your time and making the most of it, identifying and prioritising the aspects of work/study you enjoy while setting aside space for other enriching activities that make life worth living. Remember, if you're working unsociable hours and/or long shifts you should have similar time off in lieu.

(Continued)

U

Problem	Try
#Unemployment	Your support network may help you find other work, or suggest avenues for building your skills base while reassuring you of your value.

Chapter 2

#Unemployment
When I went to university academics were pretty certain they had jobs for life, and the campus was a major employer across the community.

That same university now has staff on precarious contracts and has subcontracted many key roles for cleaners, caterers and security to workers. It's happening everywhere.

Being unemployed on a short-term basis may be manageable, although only with financial safety for protection. Rent, bills and other expenses need to be paid. Aside from financial hardships, and harms caused if benefits are lacking or austerity measures are enacted, the cycle of application and rejection can take a harsh toll. Repeated periods of job seeking and/or long-term unemployment can have a devastating effect on our mental and physical health, confidence and security.

Your support network may help you find other work, or suggest avenues for building your skills base while reassuring you of your value.

You may be able to get support/training in CV writing, job applications, cover letter writing, interview skills etc from your library or online (see *Job seeking* entry), or with feedback from other colleagues. Always remember though, if you are not successful it is not for want of trying – countless people are doing all the right things and still not getting work. It may be that you want a complete career change or to find temporary work that pays the bills while you look to build your profile in other ways.

Chapter 8

The Academic Job Search Handbook 5th Edition. Julia Miller Vick, Jennifer S. Furlong and Rosanne Lurie (2016), University of Pennsylvania Press, Philadelphia.

Chapter 6

U

Problem	*Try*
#UsvsThem While collective organising, friendship and support can't solve everything, it can make lots of things bearable and bring greater results if we #StandTogether. Organisations may rely on separation to control individuals or groups; academia's fragmented design exacerbates this issue. You can be separated by subject area, place of work, theoretical standpoints, occupation, grade, or work/study status. Alongside the barriers enforced by competitiveness, back-biting and prejudice. As the late Jo Cox said in her inaugural speech to parliament in 2015 *'we are far more united and have far more in common than that which divides us'.* Many of the problems described in this chapter do not have immediate solutions. Lots of them are maintained by academic institutions because it benefits them, although not us. Individually we may struggle to make a difference or survive, but collectively we have a better chance at addressing our work/study conditions.	We can be #StrongerTogether by: Working across disciplines to strengthen our work, inspire and build friendships. Collective organising and unionising allow us to identify inequalities and campaign for rights. Supporting each other through hardships or difficult personal/ professional situations can make us stronger (see *Poverty* entry). Knowing who everyone is within your department, greeting them by name and pronouncing it correctly, and sharing breaks. Establishing events that bring everyone together regardless of role – fundraising sales, coffee mornings, potlucks, choirs, sports teams, quiz teams, gardeners, outreach groups etc. Assisting those who are in disadvantaged or dangerous situations (see *Politics and Prejudice* entry). Guide to Allyship www.guidetoallyship.com

Chapters 2 and 3

Chapter 3

Chapter 2

Chapter 7

(Continued)

V

Problem	Try
#*Violence* You may have experienced or witnessed emotional, physical, sexual or financial abuse; coercive control; stalking and harassment; online or digital abuse; or any number of these. You may be directly or indirectly affected within your own relationship or wider family, or within the workplace, including assault or abuse that happens in research settings. Alternatively, you may hear about abuse from students, colleagues or people you meet at outreach or other events (see *Safety* entry). Reading about violence within secondary data (historical records, books or court transcripts) may also be troubling. Abuse can happen to any of us. Minority and marginalised staff and students, and those who're exploited and/or unsupported within organisations may be particularly disadvantaged.	Many charities offer support via phone or email, although you may have to keep trying them as most are overstretched and underfunded. Their websites provide information on what abuse may entail, how you may react to it and what you need to put in place in order to leave an abusive relationship. A list of support organisations can be found at: https://nostartoguideme.com/if-you-need-help If you are being harmed at work you can get support from colleagues, your union and professional organisations. Human Resources should support you but, as with other kinds of bullying, their general role is to protect the reputation of the organisation so they may distance themselves from you or allow your abuser to continue or to relocate without any sanctions. This can add to the distress of the abuse you've already experienced (see *Bullying and Harassment* entry).

Chapters
3–4 and 6

V

Problem	Try
For those helping a friend or colleague in an abusive relationship remember they may struggle to leave and take several attempts before they manage it. Some people don't ever leave, either remaining in a relationship or being killed by a partner, which can leave you feeling devastated and potentially guilty that you did not do more.	If the topic of your work is triggering, particularly if you are a survivor of abuse (see NAPAC https://napac.org.uk), you can get training on managing sensitive research topics or therapy to process your reactions. This should be provided via your institution. If it isn't your union may be able to help or you may have to set up your own support system. Therapy and creating a support group of friends who're also affected is useful, see: www.nostartoguideme.com/ helpafriend Sexual Assault Network for Grads (SANG) www.ixgrads.org Faculty Against Rape www.facultyagainstrape.net End Rape on Campus (EROC) https://endrapeoncampus.org Campus Sexual Violence Resource List www.nsvrc.org/saam/ campus-resource-list The 1752 Group https://1752group.com

Chapter 6

(Continued)

W

Problem	Try

#whiteness
BIPOC readers will know whiteness all too well, but many white readers will either be unfamiliar with this term or become immediately defensive. 'White Privilege' refers to advantages white people have, but may not recognise or accept, that affects their sense of status, entitlements and opportunities. An example list by Peggy McIntosh can be found here: https://projecthumanities. asu.edu/content/ white-privilege-checklist Within academia problems of whiteness have centred on who gets to go to university or sit on panels at conferences, grant giving bodies or interviews. Who is overrepresented in senior, tenured roles? Who is more likely to be a student or continue in a research or teaching career? Whose work is credited and cited? Whose ideas

If you're a BIPOC reader, finding support from professional organisations and informal networks for scholars or workers, plus connecting on social media, may be vital in order to survive academic spaces.
White readers may find the following resources helpful in terms of understanding and addressing whiteness, along with suggestions in Chapter 3 on being an *Active bystander* (not just reading that chapter but putting the suggestions in it into action). You may also find working with white colleagues helpful to discuss and implement ideas on recognising and challenging whiteness.
Why I'm No Longer Talking To White People About Race. Reni Eddo-Lodge (2017), Bloomsbury Circus.
Showing.up for racial justice www.showingupforracialjustice.org
Anti-Racist Resources https://theresearchcompanion. com/antiracistresources
Resources for white people to learn and talk about race and racism: https://blog.fracturedatlas. org/resources-for-white- people-to-learn-and-

Chapters
1–3

W

Problem	Try
are appropriated or stolen? Who expects to be able to move freely on or off campus without being challenged or questioned? Who is better able to find accommodation, access healthcare, and receive safe and appropriate support from emergency services? Who gets to see other people who look like them?	talk-about-race-and-racism-5b207fff4fc7

Chapter 1

It can feel challenging to accept how whiteness works, excludes or harms, especially if people don't consider themselves racist – not least because it requires personal reflection, change, putting yourself into uncomfortable positions and having to address whiteness/privilege with other resistant white people.

Chapter 3, pp. 91–93

Some academic spaces have begun to interrogate and challenge whiteness in the classroom as part of white studies or other academic disciplines:

If you work in fields like #anthropology, health or #development there may be many values of #saviourship, #colonialism or #authoritarianism you need to address with other white colleagues before working in other communities; enabling local staff to lead on projects while listening to communities if they state research is not wanted, needed, nor especially helpful or ethical.

Helen Kara's *Indigenous Research Methods: A Reading List* takes you to a number of texts that challenge many of the theories and epistemologies white scholars may have been taught: https://helenkara.com/2017/07/04/indigenous-research-methods-a-reading-list

Dismantling Race in Higher Education: Racism, Whiteness and Decolonising the Academy. Jason Arday and Heidi Safia Mirza (2018), Palgrave Macmillan.

(Continued)

W

Problem	Try
within diversity training; as part of student activism; or widening participation initiatives. Problems have arisen where white people have reacted to these with anger, crying, dismissal or demanding BIPOC colleagues comfort, educate or otherwise support them. Slipping back into a position of expecting non-white people to comply, reassure, nurture and obey. Understandably, many BIPOC people are exhausted not only by everyday racism but by the lack of visible action or understanding from white students and colleagues who may be overtly racist, or more often claim not to be prejudiced while acting in countless ways that are.	
#Workload	See Chapter 7, *Creating and maintaining your boundaries*.

W

Problem	Try
#*Writing* We panic about writing, attribute huge importance to it and expect a lot to come from whatever we produce. We then get upset when it isn't noticed or is noticed for the wrong reasons. Procrastination can limit writing; as may chronic pain, disabilities, learning difficulties and exhaustion. Sometimes you run out of ideas, feel blocked or have no idea how to start.	Your organisation may offer training on grammar; essay and dissertation writing; literary techniques; storytelling; structuring work and making compelling arguments; and how to get published. Equally there are numerous guides to assist you. Experimenting with different styles and formats can help you practice your writing alongside developing your voice and noting your strengths. If you're sitting an exam or have to submit work you can use a scribe or reader (see Chapter 4 for more adjustments you may be entitled to).
If you're working in a second language, struggle physically with writing or have a learning disability, recording yourself for another person to transcribe can convey your ideas. Or you could switch to vlogging or podcasting.	You'll become a better writer through practice, feedback and reading. Who else inspires you? How do they communicate? Finding key writers you like can give you greater freedom to express yourself. Raul Pacheco-Vega has lots of practical advice on writing and note taking techniques: www.raulpacheco.org/resources

(Continued)

Z

Problem	Try
#Zerohours	Nobody will blame you for taking any work if you need the money. But joining a union and connecting with others may help you find other, more secure jobs. Chapter 2

#Zerohours
These are jobs where you're only paid for the hours you actually work, with no benefits or security, no minimum hours, no holiday pay, nor any guarantee of employment. You may have heard them called casual/sessional jobs or piece work. It can suit you if you're wanting to fit in extra work on your schedule and are otherwise financially secure, otherwise they are exceptionally risky.
These exist across academia, particularly for catering, cleaning and security staff alongside those covering teaching and marking. They are often offered with the promise that in accepting a zero hours contract, other, more secure work will follow. Sometimes this happens, often it doesn't, but people accept this either way because they have no other work, need experience or feel it might give them an advantage when seeking other work.

Nobody will blame you for taking any work if you need the money. But joining a union and connecting with others may help you find other, more secure jobs. They will also fight for your rights if you're being exploited on what's presented as a zero hours job but where your skills and responsibilities are extensive. All of us who're working in secure situations need to support those working/studying alongside us who are being exploited (see also *Poverty* and *Assessment* entries).

Chapter 2

Chapter 3

#PrecariousEmployment

That's quite a list! I'm sorry if I missed something you needed. Hopefully the resources elsewhere in this book may help; or your support network (Chapter 2) or place of work/study (Chapter 4). Remember, this book is a conversation and I will continue to blog and share advice about academia/research at www.theresearchcompanion.com and about other life stuff at www.nostartoguideme.com. If you have any recommendations for resources, support groups or other tools I can pass on, please let me know (see Chapter 8 for more information).

If this chapter has left you feeling unsettled or overwhelmed, don't worry – the next chapter focuses on how to cope if life events are affecting your physical or mental health, while Chapter 7 contains lots of gentle ideas and activities.

References

Boynton, P., 2016. *The Research Companion: A Practical Guide for the Social Sciences, Health and Development*, 2nd ed. Routledge.

6 Warning signs and symptoms

The previous chapters addressed where you can get and give help, what you need from academia and areas where people struggle. If you are living within stressful or difficult situations, regardless of whether they are inside or outside academia (or both), you may react in a variety of ways that are not always beneficial. This chapter invites you to focus on your reactions and responses and provides ideas on where to get assistance. Remember to look after yourself while working through this chapter (see *Run a diagnostic* and your *Safety plan* in Chapter 1, or skip to the end of this chapter where you'll find links to further help).

Note how many of the following symptoms currently apply to you, or have affected you for the past three months or longer, and are out of character/causing you distress.

Your symptoms (circle or shade all that apply):

sleep disturbance (insomnia, falling asleep in the day)	restlessness	fidgeting	clumsiness
distracted	difficulties concentrating	appetite changes (over/under eating)	tiredness/exhaustion
hypervigilance	increased stimming or tics	crying/feeling tearful	constantly feeling on edge
unable to relax	emotionally numb	flashbacks/upsetting memories	rehearsing/replaying events in your head
manic	agitated	irritated	angry
feeling useless or worthless	hopelessness	weight loss or gain	lethargic
hearing voices or seeing things	anxiety	depression	lack of motivation
urinary tract infections	digestive problems	nausea	stomach aches
panic attacks	increased need to pee	dry mouth	palpitations

(Continued)

thrush	reduced sexual desire/interest	temperature fluctuations (feeling very hot or cold)	recurrent ulcers
feeling like life has no meaning or purpose	believing people would be better off without you	confusion	brain fog
intrusive/negative thoughts	feeling ashamed	can't manage even basic tasks	suicidal thoughts
withdrawing from life events	avoiding people	no interest or pleasure in things you ordinarily enjoy	everything feels overwhelming/insurmountable
skin problems (acne flare-ups, eczema, rosacea)	feeling like you can't cope/can't go on	shaking/trembling	feeling dizzy or faint
memory problems	increased aches and pains	preoccupation with own/others health and safety	paranoia

There may be other symptoms/reactions you've had that aren't included above, note them here:

_____

_____

_____

_____

If you found this challenging you may need to check in with your support network; or take a break to relax or give yourself some care.
Chapter 2

Chapter 7

Having looked over these symptoms, ask yourself:

- Do I know what is happening to me, and why? Chapters 3–5
- Is this something that needs resolving (e.g. bullying) or that I need to go through (e.g. a bereavement)? Chapters 3 and 5
- Can I relieve any symptoms with information or action, or self-care? Chapters 4 and 7
- Am I able to seek and request help? If so, who can help me now? (See also your *Safety plan* in Chapter 1 and the resources at the end of this chapter.) Chapters 2–4

Write down or record your responses, or if it's easier have a trusted friend ask you questions and note your replies.

You may have numerous symptoms that aren't easily relieved but of which you know the cause. A bereavement may leave you feeling sad and angry, affect your sleep and appetite, and not be made any easier by trying to relax. But you recognise and accept these reactions as part of grief. The 'Unrecovery Star' in Chapter 3 may be worth consulting to note where there are things that cause you distress, which you understand and are unable to change but may still want support coping with.
Chapter 5

Notice the red flags of extreme symptoms for what should be everyday events. Going into work should not bring on a panic attack. Speaking to a supervisor should not make you feel sick. If you are showing negative symptoms and/or harmful coping strategies you should note what the underlying cause(s) are. From that you can then begin to seek help that will address those symptoms, your coping strategies AND the underlying causes.

Beware, too, of 'diagnostic overshadowing' – where changes in behaviour due to learning difficulties or being neurodivergent are assumed to be a physical health problem and so treated as such, as opposed to providing reasonable adjustments or mental health care (see also Cho 2019; Javaid et al. 2019); or where people with mental health issues have all of their symptoms attributed to their psychological problems, ignoring comorbidities or other physical health complaints. As you know from my story in Chapter 1 I was sick for a long time because doctors insisted that while I'd had a physical illness (Hepatitis) the majority of my symptoms (pain, digestive difficulties, sleep problems, weight loss and depression) were 'all in my head' and caused by the breakdown of my relationship. Moving house and re-registering with new doctors only added to this suspicion of my being a mad and difficult patient. As a consequence, treatment I should have been given was not provided, which meant considerable delays before I got the help I needed – all of which exacerbated my mental health problems and led to fraught future encounters with healthcare. It is hard to trust people who are supposedly there to help you but do not listen, who you have to push to take action while you are at your lowest mentally and physically, and who imply you are a problem for wanting better care. If there is one thing I learned from this it is that you have to keep pushing because if your symptoms are severe, worsening or changing, you need care! This is particularly important if you are an under-represented minority (URM), where you may already be marginalised, or you are struggling to access care, be treated with respect or taken seriously by practitioners.

Our bodies try and tell us when things are not right, but we may not heed them. Or we may be convinced by others within our work or study spaces, our home lives or even the medical profession not to listen to ourselves. Talking things over with your support network (Chapter 2) or trying the reflection exercises in Chapter 7 may allow you to notice what is going on, respond to your mental and physical reactions, and permit others to tell you how things seem to them.

Ways you may deal with distress

In Chapter 3 I talked about seeking help and the expectation that it should happen in an orderly fashion. Of course it rarely does, and the same goes for coping with problems. This is why the next section shares some of the frank ways people have told me they've attempted to deal with the symptoms listed above. There is no judgement here. Many of us have tried one or more of the following as a means of coping, or found ourselves doing them when things fell apart. If the links below don't suit your specific language, faith or other cultural needs you can ask the organisations listed if they can recommend an alternative. You can also use those you trust in your support network to seek localised resources.

Have you found yourself ...	Learn more and get assistance from ...
Drinking too much?	Club Soda https://joinclubsoda.co.uk SMART Recovery www.smartrecovery.org Life Ring https://www.lifering.org
Using drugs? (Prescription, synthetic highs or illegal substances.)	NHS advice on drug addiction www.nhs.uk/live-well/healthy-body/drug-addiction-getting-help Addiction – Sick Doctors Trust http://sick-doctors-trust.co.uk/page/addiction
Self-harming? (Picking, cutting, hair pulling etc.)	See *Venting and righteous anger* at the end of this chapter plus: Harmless www.harmless.org.uk Self Harm www.selfharm.co.uk
Putting yourself down or thinking about yourself negatively?	See *Avoiding the negativity trap* in Chapter 1 and *Stop Thinking: Start Living*. Richard Carlson (1997), Element.
Had problems with food, eating and/or body image?	Beat: Eating Disorders www.beateatingdisorders.org.uk
Lashing out at other people, starting arguments or overreacting to things that usually wouldn't bother you? Additionally, do you find yourself doing things in anger that you later regret or feeling like you don't have control over your anger in ways that may hurt you or others.	Mind Tools guide to understanding and addressing anger www.mindtools.com/pages/article/newTCS_97.htm

Being nit-picky, overly critical or difficult with yourself or other people, even though you don't want to be like this and know it's unfair?	*Embracing Your Inner Critic: Turning Self Criticism into a Creative Asset.* Hal Stone and Sidra Stone (1993), Bravo. *The Disbelief Habit: How to Use Doubt to Make Peace with Your Inner Critic.* Yong Kang Chan (2017), self-published.
Performing self-destructive, risky and self-sabotaging behaviours? (E.g. not showing up for an exam, smashing crucial equipment, drink driving.)	*Letting Go of Self Destructive Behaviours: A Workbook of Help and Healing.* Lisa Ferentz (2014), Routledge.
Procrastinating or trying to make everything perfect? Or feeling like you cannot fail.	Mind Tools guide to avoiding procrastination: www.mindtools.com/pages/article/newHTE_96.htm And understanding perfectionism: www.mindtools.com/pages/article/perfectionism.htm
Avoiding or ignoring people, or missing deadlines and key events or activities?	See Mind Tools time management resources: www.mindtools.com/pages/main/newMN_HTE.htm
Lying to cover up problem behaviour; get yourself out of situations; because you've forgotten what you were supposed to do; don't care; or want to be found out and cause a scene.	Search for 'lying' via the Mental Health charities listed at the end of this chapter.

(Continued)

Have you found yourself …	Learn more and get assistance from …
Overspending to help yourself feel better or buy the affection of others?	National Debt Advice https://nationaldebtadvice.org.uk Step Change www.stepchange.org Money Advice Service www.moneyadviceservice.org.uk Money Saving Expert www.moneysavingexpert.com Alvin Hall's tips and books https://alvinhall.com
Gambling?	Be gamble aware www.begambleaware.org Gamcare www.gamcare.org.uk Gamblers Anonymous https://gaaustralia.org.au
Displaying passive aggressive behaviour, such as telling yourself and others you're fine when you clearly aren't; or blaming others for mistakes or situations you caused?	*Overcoming Passive-Aggression: How to Stop Hidden Anger from Spoiling Your Relationships, Career and Happiness.* Tim Murphy and Lorian Oberlin (2016), De Capo Lifelong Books.
Needing support but refusing to accept it or rejecting help that would benefit you?	See *Help! I can't accept help* in Chapter 3 (pp. 75–77).
Neglecting yourself – not washing yourself or your clothes or missing meals? This may extend to not being able to look after pets or other dependents.	Manchester Safeguarding Board's Self Neglect – advice for all www.manchestersafeguardingboards. co.uk/resource/self-neglect-advice-for-all Plus see ideas for spotting a friend in crisis in Chapter 3 and Chapter 7 for gentle strategies to manage your life.

Those feelings in context

You may be reading this and thinking *'but my symptoms and reactions are appropriate!'* and you may be right – feeling paranoid if you're a victim of stalking, or being angry with a racist or sexist supervisor is understandable and people should not try to convince you otherwise. However if you're angry with a colleague because you missed a deadline they had nothing to do with, that's unfair and unreasonable and a sign you need to address what's making you so upset. Be aware that you may want to justify symptoms or responses so you don't have to acknowledge what is causing the problem or accept treatment. Sometimes it helps to sit with these feelings and be honest with ourselves, or to talk with trusted friends or support groups to get a sense of perspective. Recognising some issues may not be solved overnight or without effort, but seeking medical or therapeutic care could bring you closer to some relief. It's okay to seek help for your reactions if they're damaging you, even if they are entirely reasonable to hold.

Chapter 2

Be a psychological first aider

Psychological First Aid (PFA) is a range of tools to assist anyone affected by trauma and, like physical first aid, is designed for anyone to learn to use. It aims to help people feel supported and secure following an accident, shock or disaster; giving the option of people talking if it helps them and identifying any facilities or services that could be beneficial. At all stages those receiving PFA should feel empowered, in control and able to prioritise and attend to their own needs in their own time. My comprehensive guide to delivering PFA can be found here: https://nostartoguideme.com/psychological-first-aid (it includes free multi-age, multi-language resources).

Another approach you may have heard of is Mental Health First Aid (MHFA). This is an approach where individuals within a group or organisation are trained to work in a boundaried way to notice mental health symptoms or signs of distress; reduce mental health stigma; and deliver assistance when someone is in need of mental health support. A directory of International Mental Health First Aid organisations can be found here:

www.mhfainternational.org/international-mhfa-programs.html

Although any of us can learn PFA/MHFA (indeed these programmes are designed for lay use), not all training (or trainers) is culturally sensitive, accessible to minorities or takes a critical view on ideas like resilience or recovery. Look for accredited trainers that can offer training to suit diverse needs.

What else can you try?

Chapter 3

Pay attention to symptoms changing or worsening, or anything that concerns you (or that other people may have expressed worries over).

Seek help earlier rather than later. This is particularly important for groups that delay seeking care due to fear and mistrust, financial hardship or inaccessible services. It can affect you if you're one or more of the following:

- A shift worker/holding down several jobs.
- A man.
- Someone whose previously had bad experiences with healthcare (including anyone who's been sectioned and/or misdiagnosed).
- From the Gypsy, Roma and Traveller communities.
- Are currently homeless or in temporary accommodation.
- Are Black, Indigenous or a Person of Colour (particularly women).
- Are LGBTQ+ (particularly if you're bi and/or trans).
- Are a refugee or migrant.
- Are disabled, have a chronic illness, multiple health conditions or complex mental health needs.

(See King et al. 2003; Henry et al. 2004; Paradies et al. 2014; McKenzie-Mavinga 2016; Fenando 2017; Raifman 2018; Janz 2019)

Feeling like there is no point in seeking care is under-standable, but this makes it *all the more important that you do so*. Use your support network and advice from seeing the doctor or therapist to feel more empowered. Chapter 2

Acknowledge confusion. Feeling muddled is stressful and upsetting. Try the following to feel more settled: list what you need to do (you can always add to this as things occur to you); check regulations and syllabi and create a schedule to remind you what you should be doing, even if you can't recall why (friends/colleagues can update this for you if you're struggling); create a list of questions you want answers to or things you can't remember or aren't sure about, using your support network to get answers. If you are confused over how you feel try drawing, expressing yourself in a letter or poem, or writing a list of pros and cons. Chapter 4

Take time off, either for medical appointments, surgery, therapy sessions, check-ups, physio or other meetings; or to rest/recuperate. Chapter 4

Anticipate triggers and have a survival plan in place. If you know you are likely to struggle before or after a particular incident or event (for example finishing an essay, talking to your boss or recovering from treatment) allow yourself time to recover, have refreshments available and keep interruptions to a minimum while giving yourself what you need to feel stronger and happier. There are times when you should expect to feel pressured – when preparing for an exam, during a busy period at work that you have planned for or when interviewing for a job. And also times when you should feel distressed – after an accident or traumatic event.

Chapter 7

Chapter 1,
pp. 16–17

Look to the future. If you feel numb, depersonalised, depressed or suicidal it can be difficult to think positively about tomorrow. Using your schedule note things to anticipate, such as your birthday or other people's you care about; note how great you'll feel when a particular deadline passes; write out a wish-list of things you'd like to try; imagine you're 100 and think about what you would say in your celebratory speech.

Chapters
1 and 7

You can also *offer yourself love and care*. The next chapter will give you lots of ideas on how to do that.

Find out more

There are many organisations offering mental health advice and support, below is a selection of groups you can pick from to best suit your needs.

Mental Health

* Student Minds Mental Health Charter
  www.studentminds.org.uk/charter.html

- The Wellbeing Thesis https://thewellbeingthesis.org.uk
- The Blurt Foundation will send you regular updates and self-care guides (via phone or email): www.blurtitout.org
- The Siwe Project www.thesiweproject.org
- The Black, African and Asian Therapy network www.baatn.org.uk
- Student Minds www.studentminds.org.uk
- Recovery in the Bin https://recoveryinthebin.org
- Therapy for Black Girls www.therapyforblackgirls.com
- First Nations Mental Wellness Continuum Framework https://thunderbirdpf.org/first-nations-mental-wellness-continuum-framework
- MIND www.mind.org.uk
- SANE www.sane.or.uk
- Time To Change www.time-to-change.org.uk
- Mental Elf www.nationalelfservice.net/mental-health
- Black Thrive www.blackthrive.org.uk
- Campaign Against Living Miserably (CALM) www.thecalmzone.net
- Big White Wall www.bigwhitewall.com
- Hearing Voices Network www.hearing-voices.org
- Rethink www.rethink.org
- Anxiety UK www.anxietyuk.org.uk
- Metro (LGBT) https://metrocharity.org.uk
- Muslims Thrive https://www.muslimsthrive.org
- JAMI (Jewish Mental Health) https://jamiuk.org
- Hub of Hope https://hubofhope.co.uk
- Mental health charities in Australia: https://en.wikipedia.org/wiki/Category:Mental_health_organisations_in_Australia
- Mental health charities in Canada: https://en.wikipedia.org/wiki/Category:Mental_health_organizations_in_Canada

- Black Girls Smile list of US Mental Health resources: www.blackgirlssmile.org/resources
- Mental Health First Aid England https://mhfaengland.org
- Trauma Informed Schools (UK) www.traumainformedschools.co.uk
- Mental Health America www.mentalhealthamerica.net
- Mental Health Europe https://mhe-sme.org
- No Panic (UK) https://nopanic.org.uk
- Moodgym (Australia) https://moodgym.com.au
- Surviving Work (UK) https://survivingwork.org
- I Am Anxious In Academia https://iamanxiousinacademia.wordpress.com
- Dragonfly Mental Health http://dragonflymentalhealth.com

Physical health

- Patient.co.uk (UK) https://patient.info
- HealthTalk (UK) www.healthtalk.org
- Our Bodies, Ourselves (US) www.ourbodiesourselves.org
- Rural Health Information Hub (US) www.ruralhealthinfo.org
- CDC (US) www.cdc.gov
- NHS Live Well (UK) www.nhs.uk/live-well
- The Lowitcha Institute for Aboriginal and Torres Strait Islanders   www.lowitja.org.au/page/partnership-and-collaborations
- PACE (LGBT) www.pacehealth.org.uk

Sexual health, fertility and contraception resources can be found in Chapter 5 and relationship advice in Chapter 2, with a longer list of advice services via No Star To Guide Me: https://nostartoguideme.com/if-you-need-help

The Body Keeps the Score: Mind, Brain and Body in the Transformation of Trauma. Bessel Van Der Kolk (2014), Penguin.

You Can Do All the Things: Drawings, Affirmations and Mindfulness to Help with Anxiety and Depression. Kate Allan (2018), Mango.

The following guides address mental health issues primarily for students and include different recommendations for supporting mental wellbeing for home and international students. While from a UK perspective some of the ideas could be adapted to other country settings and from student wellbeing to that of all academic staff.

Understanding Provision for Students with Mental Health Problems and Intensive Support Needs. HEFCE (2015). https://eprints.lancs.ac.uk/id/eprint/80492/1/HEFCE2015_mh.pdf

Mental Health of Students in Higher Education. Royal College of Psychiatrists. (2011). www.rcpsych.ac.uk/docs/default-source/improving-care/better-mh-policy/college-reports/college-report-cr166.pdf?sfvrsn=d5fa2c24_2

Student Mental Health and Wellbeing in Higher Education: Good Practice Guide. www.universitiesuk.ac.uk/policy-and-analysis/reports/Documents/2015/student-mental-wellbeing-in-he.pdf

The Invisible Problem? Improving Students' Mental Health. Poppy Brown (2016), HEPI. www.hepi.ac.uk/2016/09/22/3592

Measuring Wellbeing in Higher Education. Rachel Hewitt (2019), HEPI www.hepi.ac.uk/2019/05/09/measuring-well-being-in-higher-education

The next section helps you accept and express strong emotions.

Venting and righteous anger

Many self-help guides require you to think happy thoughts and do kind things. These are important but can gloss over inequalities and disadvantages. Forcing everyone into compulsory positivity is counterproductive. There are times in life when you want – and need – to embrace 'negative' feelings and emotions. That might be rage, resentment, sadness, jealousy or fear.

As much of academia is unequal and unfair, there will be times you feel side-lined, hurt or enraged. You may also be silenced due to the way your workplace is organised, fear of losing your job, lack of support from colleagues, state control, or being treated as 'difficult' or 'strident' if you raise reasonable concerns about prejudice or inequalities.

Chapters
1 and 5

Chapters 3–5

In an ideal world you could take steps to address inequities. In reality you may not be able to bring about change, so while you are trying or looking for alternative options you may want to also do the following:

☐ Write out how you are feeling on paper or on your phone or computer (you can rip or burn the former or delete the latter for greater satisfaction; or save as evidence).
☐ Yell, scream, shout, cry or whisper.
☐ Sing songs of joy, rebellion and resistance; either alone or with a choir.
☐ Suck on an ice lolly or sip a cold drink through a straw.

☐ Rip up a newspaper, cardboard, magazine or tearable fabric.

☐ Bang a drum or tap out a rhythm on a table or box.

☐ Punch a boxing bag or pad (wear boxing gloves!); or kick/hit a cushion or soft furnishing.

☐ Swing a pillow against a wall.

☐ Paint, draw or scribble.

☐ Skim stones.

☐ Sit quietly, allowing yourself to feel strong emotions and reminding yourself these are valid responses to unfair, frustrating or dangerous situations.

☐ Make bread and really punch that dough, or really beat the batter when you make a cake.

☐ Throw ice cubes or soft fruit onto a hard floor, or watch videos of people smashing watermelons.

☐ Tidy up, do the gardening, sort through clothes, organise your cupboards, or express your fury by scrubbing your bath/shower, cooker, floors and worktops.

☐ Hold an ice cube in your hand and let it melt.

☐ Draw on your skin with washable pens or makeup.

☐ Put your hands or feet into cold water or place a wet flannel that's chilled in a fridge on your arm, leg or face.

☐ Use stress balls, fidget toys, weighted and/or comfort blankets or plushies.

☐ Sport (individual or team) and exercise classes can release tension.

☐ Watching or performing music, dance or poetry slams may allow you to release emotions and can feel healing.

☐ Direct your anger into activism and protest, awareness raising, standing together with colleagues or joining a union. As US Congressman John Lewis says, make #goodtrouble.

If you found this challenging you may be scared of sharing strong emotions – this may particularly be the case for some cultures or vulnerable minority groups. Recognising that being angry or unhappy are just as valid as other feelings is important. You may find repressing things can lead to more problems, which is why many of the ideas above are also recommended as an alternative to self-harming. If you are really concerned about your strong feelings seek professional help (particularly if you feel suicidal, see *Safety plan*, Chapter 1). Otherwise, the alternative, gentler activities in Chapter 7 may better suit your needs.

References

Cho, H.L., 2019. Can Intersectionality Help Lead to More Accurate Diagnosis? *The American Journal of Bioethics* 19, 37–39.

Fenando, S., 2017. *Institutional Racism in Psychiatry and Clinical Psychology: Race Matters in Mental Health.* London: Palgrave Macmillan.

Henry, B.R., Houston, S., Mooney, G.H., 2004. Institutional Racism in Australian Healthcare: A Plea for Decency. *Medical Journal of Australia* 180, 517–520.

Janz, H.L., 2019. Ableism: The Undiagnosed Malady Afflicting Medicine. *CMAJ* 191, E478.

Javaid, A., Nakata, V., Michael, D., 2019. Diagnostic Overshadowing in Learning Disability: Think beyond the Disability. *Progress in Neurology and Psychiatry* 23, 8–10.

King, M., McKeown, E., Warner, J., Ramsay, A., Johnson, K., Cort, C., Wright, L., Blizard, R., Davidson, O., 2003. Mental Health and Quality of Life of Gay Men and Lesbians in England and Wales: Controlled, Cross-sectional Study. *British Journal of Psychiatry* 183, 552–558.

McKenzie-Mavinga, I., 2016. *The Challenge of Racism in Therapeutic Practice: Engaging with Oppression in Practice and Supervision*, 2nd ed.. London: Palgrave.

Paradies, Y., Truong, M., Priest, N., 2014. A Systematic Review of the Extent and Measurement of Healthcare Provider Racism. *Journal of General Internal Medicine* 29, 364–387.

Raifman, J., 2018. Sanctioned Stigma in Health Care Settings and Harm to LGBT Youth. *JAMA Pediatrics* 172, 713–714.

7 Looking after yourself

So far this book has focused on what's going on around you, coping strategies, how to support others and seeking assistance. This chapter covers tips and techniques others have recommended to help you help yourself. Not all of these will appeal (see *A slice of advice* in Chapter 1), but all are designed to be adapted to suit your needs and shared with others who might benefit from them; or to inspire you to seek out even more self-care ideas or create ones of your own.

Meet the CLANGERS

I don't mean the cute space puppets created 50 years ago for BBC Children's Television by Oliver Postgate and Peter Firmin, but rather a list of things of which you should include one or more of each day to bring routine and relief (New Economics Foundation 2008; Hammond 2018). You'll see these ideas echoed across this chapter and elsewhere in the book. Share yours on social media using #CLANGERS4ALL.

CONNECT – touch base with others. Let people know their work moved you; join a social media chat; reach out to someone who's struggling.

LEARN – try a new skill, take a course, listen to a podcast.

ACTIVITY – that may be gentle exercises (see below), or other forms of fitness and sport.

NOTICE – what is happening around you? Anything different or unusual, or something you'd ordinarily overlook?

GIVE BACK – friendship, volunteering or outreach can help you feel better and more purposeful – and make the world that little bit nicer.

EAT – being nourished gives you more energy, helps fight some infections and allows you to better manage medical care.

RELAX – You get to decide what 'rest' is like for you. For some people it requires no interruptions, for others it's about more time to lie down and/or sleep. Others can rest while listening to music, a podcast or story; cooking or crafting; or prefer a guided meditation in a class or app. Let whatever method of relaxation you pick bring you to a more comfortable place to gather yourself.

SLEEP – you need sleep for health, growth, energy and concentration, particularly if you're struggling with mental or physical health issues or experiencing a lot of stress. Sleep problems are often linked to other worries or pain, and not being able to sleep can become a source of stress in itself. Learning patterns of sleep hygiene can leave you better placed to deal with the day ahead.

Find out more

Phil Hammond's CLANGERS for all, every day
www.drphilhammond.com/blog/2018/09/18/health4all/2593
The National Sleep Foundation www.sleepfoundation.org

Do nice, Be Kind, Spread Happy: Acts of Kindness for Kids. Bernadette Russell (2014), Ivy Press.

Pass it on

For those of you on campuses or working within organisations that have regular terms/phases there will be annual leftovers – books, folders, clothing, equipment, crockery, bedding etc. Lots of this could be collected and repurposed for new students, staff or the wider community. Organise collection points for people to drop off items in clean/good condition, then distribute at the start of the new academic year. You can also do swaps – bringing in clean clothes, unused toiletries or books to share. Or collate unwanted but usable items for a charity/jumble sale in aid of a good cause. Skills can also be traded – cooking, cleaning, mending and tutoring.

Just do it!

Chapter 2, p. 94

While thinking ahead and planning are important skills sometimes you just need to *start something*. This may feel counterintuitive if you are unsure what to do, what steps to take or where to begin. You can get trapped by believing you have to have a clear starting point or goal, meaning you don't make any progress. Instead, try beginning by reading/listening to a book, downloading an application form or calling a friend.

If you found this challenging it may be because routines and structure drive your work or help you feel comfortable. If it's really uncomfortable to get started, a very clear break from studying or work may leave you more refreshed and focused.

Getting stuff done

If you're feeling overwhelmed it's easy to fall behind, get stuck or have no idea where to begin. While there are resources to guide you on the organisation of everything from household clutter to study skills, I've found a *'do what you can today'* approach accessible and achievable. Chapter 5 This accounts for time, budget, energy levels, mobility, support, personal history/background and enthusiasm. Chapter 3 It also means you do *something*, which may be entirely adequate to suit your needs or may encourage you to take on one more thing.

Here's how it works. Consider what's going on in your life or the tasks you have to do. Break these down into small parts, then do the smallest thing. For example, *I need to freshen up* begins with the minimum action of washing. But that may be too much. Instead you might consider:

- using baby wipes on any sweaty areas
  - or
- a strip wash using soap and a flannel
  - or
- taking a shower or bath
  - then
- drying off and putting on fresh clothes.

Each of these requires time and energy, but all will leave you feeling refreshed. You decide which is feasible for you today. Make a note of the tasks you need to do for your personal hygiene, work/study and home life. Break these down to daily, weekly, monthly activities, then ask 'what can I cut?', 'what can I keep to a minimum?', 'what can I get help with?', 'what can I delegate?'. If the starting point or action is overwhelming or off-putting thinking about the outcome may be more motivating. When I'm exhausted the thought of a shower is a chore not a treat, but I know I'll feel so much better if I have one.

Chapters 2 and 4

If you found this challenging and have been struggling to find good in any part of life it might be an indicator you need additional help from your doctor, therapist or support group. I can usually make myself get on with work, exercise, cooking and bathing, but I know when these move from self-care to a chore, and then to personal neglect, it's time to seek outside help.

Chapters 2 5 and 6

Everyday rituals

These are small activities you do to reward yourself and remind yourself you are valued. Others have recommended:

- Making tea or coffee in a pot and taking time to pour on the boiled water, smell the leaves/grounds brewing, then tip slowly into a favourite cup.
- Warming facial oil in your hand, inhaling if it's scented and smoothing it gently over your face.
- Applying conditioner to your hair or a face mask to your skin and relaxing for a while as it takes effect.
- Enjoying the look/feel/sound of pen on paper.
- Meditation, reflection or prayer.

Reinforce the little things you do by telling yourself you're grateful for them; this in turn might let you acknowledge more good things and foster a positive outlook.

Dodge the disappointment trap

If negative events have been going on for a long time you can get stuck in a cycle of despair. You can't see any positives. Negatives are both distressing and familiar. For a long time bad things were happening to me in quick succession, many of which I had zero control over. In situations like this it's understandable for us to feel low, but it can also become a habit and a superstition – as so much bad stuff is happening we daren't hope for anything good lest that goes wrong too. At a time when I was feeling particularly hopeless I read a tip in a magazine (the details of which I unfortunately don't recall). It encouraged anyone trapped in a cycle of disappointment to strategically change how they start their day – to resist assuming it would automatically be negative and give themselves permission to find a little bit of joy somewhere. Then to challenge the belief that in allowing yourself hope you were inviting disaster by noting each day you managed to do this and it didn't all go wrong, and telling yourself that you deserve good things. I found it hard to do, but over time it became easier. While there is so much I can't change (see the Unrecovery star in Chapter 3) I recognised it didn't mean I deserved everything to be sad and difficult, so I could be brave and try to be a bit happier, day by day.

Chapter 1

Set your own schedule

When you're encouraged to manage your time, diarise or plan, traditionally you're expected to prioritise work/study. Resist this by first scheduling your breaks – holidays and other downtime across the weeks/months/year. Next add hobbies, interests and whatever brings you pleasure. Include reminders for birthdays or other important occasions, plus a note to call/email loved ones. Then add household chores; plus slots for meals, bathing or showering. If you have dependents include their schedule with yours, ensuring everyone knows what is going on and it doesn't fall to you to do the emotional labour and keep everyone's schedule in your head! Note key points arising through the week/month/year that you need to join (meetings, exams, workshops, training), which may apply both to your work/study in academia and events happening outside it (for example doctor's appointments or a relative's show). You might try scheduling software or diary tools to keep track of your time, such as:

Chapter 5

Daylio https://daylio.webflow.io
Todoist https://todoist.com
Panda Planner https://pandaplanner.com
Passion Planner https://passionplanner.com
The Circle Planner https://paperdesign.co
Work Flowy https://workflowy.com

At the end of each week/month reflect and see how you got on, making a commitment to prioritise the positive, and rescheduling anything that you forgot or that has fallen behind. While at the end of every day you could try #3goodthings that happened today:
1. Dodged a rain shower. 2. Heard a song I love on the radio. 3. Watched seagulls soaring over the sea.

1. Felt the sun on my face. 2. Caught up with my favourite TV series. 3. Played with my friend's kitten.

These are examples of 'three good things' (see Seligman et al. 2005; Sheldon and Lyubomirsky 2006; Pietrowsky and Mikutta 2012; Cunha et al. 2019), where noting what you're grateful or happy about is supposed to increase feelings of wellbeing and encourage a hopeful outlook. Pooky Knightsmith https://www.youtube.com/pookyh has created a social media friendly version using #3goodthings that you can join in with.

If you found this challenging this exercise favours those that have time, energy and a life that allows for happiness. You may still find it a useful reminder that during loss, abuse or other stress, there is hope. You have the right to find beauty, dignity and joy in life. Remember, it is perfectly fine to avoid this activity if you want to grieve, be angry or vent in other ways.

Chapter 6,
pp. 208–210

Reviewing your week

At the end of each week ask yourself:

- What did I like/what good things happened?
- What am I looking forward to in the coming seven days?
- What would I like to change or do differently?

You might share these questions as part of a family, house or departmental meeting, or swap answers with friends or record them in a diary. Some people refer to this exercise as 'rose, thorn, bud'. Where roses are what's gone well, thorns are problems or barriers, and buds are things you're anticipating or developing.

Regular routines

What do you do daily or weekly to help you feel in control? A sense of structure can be reassuring, particularly if you're neurodiverse or are managing multiple needs, appointments, medications etc. If you are very busy, unwell or distressed, a routine makes the best use of your time or brings order to an unstructured life. Having a list to work through, even if you feel like you are on autopilot, can be better than frantically trying to remember what you should be doing. You can also be motivated by a routine on days when you don't feel inclined to do anything.

This might include:

- Setting out your clothes, ensuring your bag is packed or any work/study equipment is ready, and a lunch is prepared the night before.
- Having a morning or evening wash.
- Ensuring you know your travel route.
- Noting what tasks will be on your agenda across the day.

Chapter 4 provides ideas for making work/study easier and these could be incorporated into your routines checklist. Remember that routines, while giving us structure, also give us permission to make occasional tweaks that can be equally pleasurable. A cancelled meeting/tutorial might be a great opportunity to relax, have a snack or enjoy a book. Deciding to do something off-schedule can help you feel mischievous or free. Equally, if you are most comfortable with extremely clear instructions and routines, having a Plan B for when things might not go to schedule can reduce your anxiety and avoid wasting your time.

Change your routine

Get up half an hour earlier or later. Have fruit or yoghurt instead of toast or cereal and listen to a different radio station while you eat breakfast. Take an alternative route to work; or find a hotel, café or library to work in. Have your lunch in the park, meet a friend to share your food with or spend time listening to music. Go home earlier or later. Eat a meal you usually wouldn't try, or a favourite dish in a different part of your home. If you ordinarily watch TV before bed, read a book or listen to music. If you usually stay home alone, call a friend or go out for the evening. You only need to make one small change to feel things are different from the usual rut.

Find out more

The HappySelf Journal, written and published by Francesca Geens (2018). Instagram @happyselfjournal

Confidence. The Journal: Your Year of Positive Thinking. Katie Piper (2018), Quercus.

The Wellbeing Journal: Creative Activities to Inspire. In aid of MIND (2017), Michael O'Mara Books.

Ryder Carroll's Bullet Journal:
https://bulletjournal.com

The School of Life have a range of products including cards, books and games focusing on affirmations, calmness, kindness and gratitude:
www.theschooloflife.com/shop/games-kits
I can cards
https://icancards.co.uk

Natalie Costa's Power Cards (designed for children but useful for adults too): www.powerthoughts.co.uk

Creating and maintaining boundaries

Saying no

'No is a complete sentence' is a well-known phrase attributed to author Anne Lamott, and a useful reminder that a one word response is often all we need. We're expected to say yes to opportunities, instructions and requests. Especially those from minority groups or in precarious situations who may need to be agreeable as a survival skill, facing hostility or harm if they refuse to co-operate. Saying no can be an important means of protecting your boundaries, energy, feelings and time. You might say no to an event, task or project; refuse to support another colleague's inappropriate behaviour; or ensure you don't work over your allocated/paid for time. Sarah Ahmed discusses this far more eloquently here: https://feministkilljoys.com/2017/06/30/no (see also Ahmed 2017; Lorde 2018).

Chapter 5

#digitaldowntime

Block out time (an hour, half day, evening) where you will have no access to games, your phone, computer etc. Then do something else you love such as reading a book or cooking your favourite food. Perhaps include friends or family in this – taking a walk, playing a board game or watching TV together. After one or more of these sessions reflect on what positive things you gained.

Remember, you're in control of your gadgets and games so can set times where you can't access the Internet or can limit phone or computer use. For example:

- No tech an hour before bed.
- No phones at the table/during meals.
- Use airplane mode to reduce distractions.
- Turn off the wifi.
- Work in places where there is no wifi.
- Establish a 'no gadget' or quiet work area.
- Leave your devices switched off or in another room while you're focusing on a task.

And if you use your phone to get you up in the morning, invest in an old fashioned alarm clock!

These apps have also been recommended for restricting phone use:

Forest www.forestapp.cc
Freedom https://freedom.to
StayFocusd www.stayfocusd.com
Self Control https://selfcontrolapp.com
Cold Turkey https://getcoldturkey.com

Nourish yourself

Skipping meals, not feeling like you deserve to eat or not being able to afford food are all harmful. When you're stressed or busy you can forget to eat but may also not have the time, budget or energy to cook from scratch. Noting time for shopping, preparing, cooking and eating food is important (see *Set your own schedule* above) and gives you permission to feed yourself as well as you would a friend or relative you care about. Taking turns to cook for friends/loved ones, batch cooking, using ready-made meals or food delivery services may help.

Find out more

British Heart Foundation Recipe Finder
www.bhf.org.uk/informationsupport/support/healthy-living/healthy-eating/recipe-finder
Diabetes UK Enjoy Food
www.diabetes.org.uk/guide-to-diabetes/enjoy-food
Tin Can Cook. Jack Monroe (2019), Bluebird.
NHS Get Fit For Free
www.nhs.uk/live-well/exercise/free-fitness-ideas

Create a hydration station

Whether you're working/studying in or outside the home, make a space for cups and straws and fill a jug, flask or bottle with water. Make things more refreshing by chilling the water and adding ice cubes, mint leaves, lemon or lime slices, or dilute with juice.

Switch off social media

Social media can be a lifeline – a means to learn, stay connected or just look at cat pictures. Unfortunately, it can also be a place for bullying, harassment, abuse, unchecked prejudice and exposure to all kinds of messages that can make you feel anxious, insecure, depressed and inadequate. You may find yourself checking in to your social media accounts right before bed, making it difficult to relax and sleep. Or tuning in first thing in the morning, setting the tone for the rest of your day. Limiting time spent on social media can greatly reduce the negative aspects. Remember *'You can be woke without waking to the news'* (Kleon 2019, p. 44).

Chapters 1, 3, 5 and 6

Change your SO/ME to So, Me?

- Have specific times during a day/week when you use social media.
- Use automated posts for news you want to share.
- Note particular issues that sap your energy and avoid conversations that cause you distress or waste your time.
- Mute or block individuals or words/phrases that exhaust or upset you.
- Reflect on how social media leaves you feeling – energised or enraged?
- If you access social media via your phone check how much time you are spending on it, and compare that with the time you put into other activities.
- Seek out positive stories or follow people who leave you feeling uplifted.

Chapters 1,
3 and 5

If you found this challenging it might be because much of what is played out on social media is a part of your daily life – facing prejudice and abuse, living within poverty, or otherwise marginalised. Social media may be a survival strategy for you to stay informed about issues that are vital for your safety. If you are facing difficulties offline *and* online, however, limit what you *can* control – the time you spend on social media and what you follow

Chapters 6

there, while trying to take steps to keep yourself as safe as possible offline. Alternatively you may feel inadequate or anxious while using social media, yet cannot stop tuning in (aka doomscrolling) either because you're trapped in a self-comparison spiral or your work demands you stay connected (or both). If this is the case concentrate on the benefits, such as sharing your ideas, being kind and building knowledge.

Be inspired

Get motivated by song lyrics; lines from poems, novels or religious texts; or ideas shared by people you admire. You might want to print out or download inspirational quotes, buy ready-made artwork with uplifting phrases or make your own. Host an *inspiration event* with friends or colleagues using collage, quote and image sharing, or sewing to create something beautiful for you to display in your office, home or on your phone.

If you found this challenging it may be because of time, energy or budget constraints that make you feel like you can't create something. There are plenty of examples regularly shared online though that you can store and return to if they resonate with you; some of these are listed at the end of Chapter 6.

Wear your heart on your sleeve

You can get pins, badges, scarves and other apparel that share positive messages or represent science, the arts or #activism. These can be great conversation starters and can also signify you're a safe person to connect with (e.g. a rainbow flag pin). You may want to customise your work pass or conference badge with stickers, hashtags sharing work you're involved with or groups you're part of, along with #hellomynameis inspired by the late Kate Granger www.hellomynameis.org.uk to encourage us all to let others we're working with know who we are, while teaching and caring more compassionately.

Find out more

Two Photon Art https://twophotonart.com
The Stem Squad Store https://thestemsquad.com
Svaha https://svahausa.com
Mutha Hood https://muthahoodgoods.com
Punky Pins https://punkypins.co.uk
Doodle Cats www.doodlecatsshop.co.uk
Science With Style www.sciencewithstyle.org
The Stylish Academic https://stylishacademic.com

Make a #playlist

Music can leave us feeling energised, comforted or emboldened. It can lift us up or help us wind down. You can listen to different playlists to match your moments and mood created by music streaming apps like Spotify,

YouTube Music, Amazon Music or Grooveshark, or you can compile your own playlists on iTunes. You might want to share or co-create with loved ones. Some events and conferences or project launches now come with their own playlist! How about an entrance song to play for yourself before you take a class, give a talk or go for an interview?

Stitch and bitch, knit and kvetch

#Crafting collectives have been part of women's lives for generations, passing on patterns and techniques for #beadwork, #embroidery, #knitting, #woodwork, #jewellery making, #felting, #crochet, #sewing, #weaving, #pottery and #patchwork. Increasingly people of all genders are finding ways to learn new things and preserve familial or indigenous patterns and techniques while connecting with others on crafty lunches, nights or weekend courses. You might want to join or establish a group, perhaps working together on projects, or sharing skills and food. This might involve making items for hospitals, care homes, food banks or other charities, such as toys, baby clothing, blankets or mending clothes for low-income adults. Some people also find crafting helps their concentration, or reduces anxiety or feelings of panic.

Find out more

How To Be a Craftivist: The Art of Gentle Protest. Sarah Corbett (2017), Unbound.

Craft Activism: People, Ideas and Projects From the New Community of Handmade and How You Can Join In. Joan Tapper and Gale Zucker (2011), Potter Craft.

Guerrilla Kindness and Other Acts of Creative Resistance: Making A Better World Through Craftivism. Sayraphim Lothian (2018), Mango.

Craftivist Collective https://craftivist-collective.com

Woolly Hugs www.woollyhugs.org

@IndigenousBeads rocur account on Twitter.

The following hashtags can help you find other crafters, patterns, requests for #handmade items, plus can provide you with the opportunity to support and purchase people's work.

#beadwork #IndigenousArt #MétisArt #MétisBeadwork #NativeArt #NativeBeadwork #embroideryart #bordado #broderie #screenprinting #crossstitch #needlework #amigurumi #yarn #ganchillo #hechoamano #diy #makersgonnamake #knittersoftheworld #strikk #knittersgonnaknit

Chill out cafe

Chapters 1 and 2 discussed ways of connecting with other people and you can extend this with specific gatherings to help people relax or reduce stress. This may be a weekly or monthly gathering, either at work or in a local café, community centre or faith-based venue, where attendees can either take it in turns to prepare food or bring their own snacks. Some universities already host these, while other events are organised informally by individuals or cafes or through mental health groups. You can use these events simply to socialise or unwind if you're feeling stressed or exhausted; organise for speakers to tackle mental health issues at such meetings; or provide pleasant activities that allow people to connect through cooking, crafting or comedy. Book clubs can also function in this way, as do 'friendship tables' in cafés or 'friendship benches' strategically placed outside libraries or other communal spaces, which indicate the people sitting there would like to be joined by someone else. You can learn more on how to join or establish an activity like this via Frazzled Café (UK) www.frazzledcafe.org and Friendship Bench (Zimbabwe) www.friendshipbenchzimbabwe.org.

Make time to relax

One object, two minutes, eight steps

You can use this exercise to focus your attention, which in turn can be calming if you are struggling with panic or other anxiety symptoms.

1 Pick up or look at an item that's within your sight/reach (e.g. an ornament, a piece of clothing, a cushion or toy, a shell or a flower).
2 Close your eyes and feel the object – is it soft or hard, spiky or smooth? Turn it in your hand and see how many ways you can experience it by touch and/or sight – what colour is it? What texture? Does the colour change if you move the object around?
3 Sniff the object – does it smell of anything?
4 If it's not likely to harm you, you could lick or taste the object. Or softly rub it on your lips or cheek.
5 If it won't break the object, give it a shake – does it make a noise? If you press it by your ear can you hear anything?

6   Weigh it in your hand – is it heavy or light? How does it feel? Is it fragile or durable? What kind of size is it – small, medium or large?

7   Think about the object. What words can you use to describe it? How many different adjectives? What uses might it have? Who would like or dislike it? What other stories might it tell?

8   Set the object down. Consider all the things you have learned about it in a short time. Do you see it differently? Was there something you discovered about it that you didn't know before?

The aim of this exercise is to help calm you and illustrate how any object might have hidden things that you wouldn't necessarily notice without attention (see the 'N' in CLANGERS above). This can help you focus and slow down with other areas of your work/life, as well as allow you to appreciate that you, also, may have lots of hidden aspects yet to be revealed.

Get physical

Try this as a distraction, to help you feel calmer, or as a break that may be necessary if you have spent periods concentrating, sitting or standing. Adapt these based on your physical ability and comfort. Ignore anything that is difficult or physically or mentally painful. Stop if you feel dizzy or anything hurts. Most of these can be done prone or seated, others require you to stand.

Jazz hands – shake or wave your hands, rotate your wrists clockwise and anti-clockwise. Clap. Wriggle your fingers.

Action arms – raise your arms to the side, to the front and above your head. Stretch or wave your arms in the air. Swing your arms forwards and back, adding a clap in front and behind you.

Neck rolls – tilt your head gently downwards so your chin is pointing towards your chest, then slowly roll it back so you are looking upwards. Repeat this a few times before gently looking to the left, then the right. If it's comfortable you can roll your head from the right downwards, then to the left and upwards – repeat.

Face time – gently close and open your eyes. Blink rapidly a few times. Raise and lower your eyebrows. Wriggle your nose. Open and close your mouth. Yawn. Smile.

Toe taps – either seated or standing, tap the toes of your right foot gently to the floor. Then place your foot flat. Do the same with your left foot and alternate for several repetitions. You can add in lifting your foot from the heel, so your toes come off the floor. You can either do this foot by foot, (if seated or standing) or both feet together (if seated). Wriggle your toes. Stomp your feet on the floor. Lift each foot off the floor gently, then replace. Circle your ankles clockwise and anti-clockwise.

Leg work – extend your leg from the knee or from the hip (this can be done seated or standing, and with support for balance). Slowly lift and lower. Try lifting your leg to the front, taking it slowly out to the side and then to the back before bringing it back to standing. Bounce gently from the knees. Jump up and down. Hop. Run on the spot. Try star jumps.

You can also combine some of these activities. For example, try sitting down and rotating your wrists and ankles at the same time – making it more of a challenge by trying opposite hands and feet; jumping while shaking out your hands; or gently wriggling your fingers and toes. These activities can be as gentle or strong as you wish. You can do them for a brief period or incorporate all of these into a routine you fit into your schedule; or for self-regulation. Some people like to do them to music – either soothing music for gentle stretches or energetic music to get you going. Others like to focus on each part they're exercising, complimenting and affirming their body, and giving themselves a soothing pat or rub afterwards.

#relax

Many academic organisations host #relaxation or #mindfulness classes. *These are only useful if whatever is causing the need for students and staff to have these sessions is also addressed.* Alongside work/study events you might explore directed relaxation activities, either online or via audiobooks, or take a course to learn how to meditate. Below is a selection of tools to help you, particularly for when using relaxation or mindfulness if you are anxious or stressed. Note that while some people find mindfulness, relaxation and #meditation powerful and positive, others experience them as uncomfortable, triggering or distressing, in which case stop immediately and explore other options for self-care. Instructions on how to practice mindfulness can be found at http://bemindful.co.uk, while Moodjuice have a number of guides on relaxation, audio guides on coping with a variety of mental health issues and mindfulness resources:

Chapters 1, 3 and 4

www.moodjuice.scot.nhs.uk/relaxation.asp
www.moodjuice.scot.nhs.uk/asppodcast.asp
www.moodjuice.scot.nhs.uk/mildmoderate/
MindfulnessDownloads.asp. You can also try Calm
www.calm.com or Insight Timer https://insighttimer.com

Poems on prescription

If you find poetry uplifting or inspiring you can sign up to the Poetry Foundation's free *Poem of the Day* service where they'll email you a daily dose of poetry based around different seasonal themes: www.poetryfoundation.org/poems/poem-of-the-day. Alternatively, Reading Well curates a list of Books On Prescription for a variety of issues to buy or order from your library: https://reading-well.org.uk/books/books-on-prescription.

Explore your senses

Focusing on our senses can allow us to experience the world differently and be a means of relaxation or distraction. If one or more of your senses are impaired you may want to focus on others, trying the suggestions below.

Taste – sweet or sour? Spicy or plain? Hot or cold? What taste sensations and flavours do you enjoy?

Smell – creosote, petrol, coffee and freshly baked bread are my favourite smells. The smell of Camay soap reminds me of warm hugs from my grandmother. What are your favourite smells and what happy memories can certain smells trigger for you?

Sound – what can you hear when you shut your eyes and listen carefully? If you play a piece of music and focus intensely on that, how much more can you appreciate it?

Sight – a beautiful sunset, petals on a flower, films of kittens padding their paws. What images make you feel happy, amazed, energised?

Touch – what feels nice to wear, fiddle with or hold? It might be fabric, a shell, fidget device, blanket or plushie.

Using one or more of your senses together, take five minutes to:

Look around you – what can you **see**? Check the first three things you notice, or search for something specific like how many things of a particular colour you can spot. How many animals, cars, plants etc?

What can you **feel**? That may be the warm sun on your body or a cold wind on your face. If there are any objects near you, you could pick them up and note their weight and texture – how might a soft cushion compare with a glass paperweight?

Birdsong, a car driving past in the rain, the wind buffeting your windows, children playing outside. What can you **hear**? How do the sounds around you change depending on the time of day, changing seasons and where you are located?

Your nose might pick up the scent of freshly cut grass, coffee brewing in the pot, fresh bread straight out of the oven or a really stinky cheese to go on that warm loaf. What can you **smell**?

If you eat that bread or stinky cheese how does it **taste**? Take a little more time to look at, smell, feel and then savour the food you are eating. If you are on a restricted or liquid diet you might eat without paying much attention to the process, so slowing down and noting tastes, even if it's the same food as usual, could be worth exploring. Or, if your diet/ability/allergies permit, you could dab mint, lemon or other strong but pleasant flavours onto the tip of your tongue.

If you're in need of a **rapid intervention** to reduce panic and self-regulate you can use the senses you're aware of with the 5, 4, 3, 2, 1 activity:

- Five things you can see.
- Four things you can feel.
- Three things you can hear.
- Two things you can smell (or think about two favourite smells).
- One thing you can taste (or one kind thing you can tell yourself).

Use this to pause and connect with your surroundings. If you are unable to see or hear you could focus instead on what you can feel or smell (or vice versa). The idea of this exercise is to calm yourself by becoming more aware of your surroundings, distracting you from anxiety or panic. It's a relatively easy and unobtrusive activity you can do in varied locations – perhaps comparing what you experience in one place (outside in the park) to another (in a café). You can always return to this, remembering how particular things felt, smelt, tasted and so on. Or use the resources listed at the end of Chapter 6 if you are feeling particularly panicky, anxious or depressed.

Reconnect with nature

You can try the following activities in person or watching films online to feel more connected with the world around you:

#BirdWatching
#BeachCombing
Quiet time in the #woods
#BugSpotting
#PondDipping
#CloudWatching

#StarGazing
#WeatherForecasting
#Nature tours/walks
Watching films, reading nature books/guides or search-
ing for social media naturists
Guided sessions/nature talks
Looking at films/photos you took in the past, or that others
have taken, if you can't currently access outside spaces
Sit #outside for lunch/dinner
Take advantage of any conferences offering tours of local
scenery or #wildlife.

Find out more

The Walker's Guide to Outdoor Clues and Signs. Tristan
Gooley (2014), Sceptre.
  *Mindfulness and the Natural World: Bringing Our
Awareness Back to Nature*. Claire Thompson (2018),
Leaping Hare Press.
  Birdsong Radio (Royal Society for the Protection of
Birds – RSPB) www.rspb.org.uk/get-involved/campaigning/
let-nature-sing/birdsong-radio
  #walking #nature #hiking #travel #landscape #trekking
#explore #mountains #outdoors #forest #sea #sky.

Gardening

Maintaining a garden and watching things grow can have
several positive effects. It's a skill to learn – particularly
finding out about how to cultivate different plants and
help them grow successfully; and focuses your attention

on digging, weeding, planting, pruning or harvesting. It can attract wildlife to your garden, which you can enjoy watching and feeding. Or you may like to have a green space for you to read or relax in. Consider:

- A #WildlifeGarden or #meadow that attracts #bees, #butterflies, #birds, #bats or other animals.
- A #windowbox or pots for #flowers, small #trees or #vegetables.
- A campus or workplace communal garden that's maintained collectively by students and staff, creating a shared space for relaxation or food for the community.
- An #allotment you tend alone or share.
- A #SensoryGarden where different scented and textured #herbs and #plants can be enjoyed by everyone, and especially those who are blind or partially sighted.
- A terrarium.
- A #SandGarden, which may contain no plants at all but can be raked and shaped and can include small stones to decorate, all of which can be a peaceful ritual for you to use to unwind.

Find out more

Thrive: Carry On Gardening www.carryongardening.org.uk
The Green Scheme www.greenscheme.org
Gardening The Community
www.gardeningthecommunity.org
RHS Set up a community garden
www.rhs.org.uk/get-involved/community-gardening/
resources/community-garden

Plants for a sensory garden
https://schoolgardening.rhs.org.uk/resources/info-sheet/plants-for-a-sensory-garden

#CommunityGarden #gardening #UrbanFarm #LearninGardens #FoodAccess #EnvironmentalJustice #FoodJustice #UrbanAgriculture #GreenScheme #CampusGarden #CityGarden #LocalFood #FoodForest

Treat time

Stop and break throughout your day using some of the activities described above, and prioritising drinks and snacks. Take time to acknowledge what you've got done and encourage yourself to take on another task. You can also set yourself bigger rewards – a prize for getting through the week might be an evening to yourself, watching your favourite TV shows or enjoying a meal with friends. Or you may want to save for something – a book, holiday, concert, artwork, jewellery, makeup or clothing – earned at the end of finishing a chapter or getting a promotion. Just for fun you could give yourself a sticker or make yourself a certificate of awesomeness.

If you found this challenging it may be because you feel unsupported elsewhere – in which case it's even more important to give yourself treats. If your workplace doesn't do it, give it to yourself. As food and drink are vital needs it can be counterproductive to make these into special rewards when they are a necessary part of your day. If you're unsure how to reward yourself think about what kindnesses you would show a friend, then give yourself the same.

Chapter 2,
pp. 41–42

Be a kid again

How often do you #play? Fly a #kite? Squish some #playdoh? Do a #jigsaw puzzle? #Colour in? Kick or catch a ball? #Skip? Demolish a #jenga tower or build with #lego? Play can be soothing. Funny. A good distraction from life's worries and a reminder of simpler times. What games did you like to play when you were younger that you could try again now? Remember resources made for kids can also be fantastic for adults too – like Bucket Fillers https://bucketfillers101.com

Where's your happy place?

It might be a geographical location you've visited. Perhaps it's very near where you live now, somewhere you visited as a child, or have never been to but have seen in photos or films. It might be a real or fantasy location.

- How does it smell?
- How does it sound?
- How does it feel?
- Is it day or night?
- Is it warm or cold?
- What legends or stories does it hold?
- Who is there with you?
- What do you do there?

If it is somewhere you can easily reach in person then take time to identify and visit your happy place. It might be a room in your house, a place at work, or another location.

Or it might be something in your memory or imagination in which case go there regularly via drawing, books, films or daydreams.

Create a self-care menu

What small things bring you pleasure? People tell me they enjoy:

bubble baths	listening to music	face masks	scented candles
binge watching TV	staying in bed	early nights	putting on pyjamas as soon as you get in
playing with pets	reading magazines	going for walks	day spa
browsing Instagram	seeing friends	bike rides	getting a massage

You might want to use some or all of these to make your own menu to select from when you want some quality downtime.

Praise yourself

Positive Post-its – Write affirming messages to yourself and leave them around your home or stuck into books.

Send yourself a postcard – whenever you go away write yourself a message about something good you've enjoyed or experienced, then mail it so it's waiting when you get home.

Your feel-good folder – save positive emails or social media compliments. Dip in whenever you need a boost, want to remind yourself of your achievements or value, or need to provide endorsements of your work or publicise what you do. You can also add photos of you working or having fun, or keep other records as reminders (I've kept all the nice references I've ever received).

This is your celebration – how often do you celebrate yourself? Not as often as you should, I'm guessing. Here are some ways to recognise the things you do:

1 Look back over the past few weeks, months or year and note key things that you did that make you feel pleased and proud.
2 Keep a regular check on what you've achieved, taking time to praise and reward yourself.

Things you might include are sticking at a task and getting it done, making a difference to someone else, hitting a milestone or quitting something that wasn't working. Or noting when you tried something new (especially if it felt scary or you didn't believe you could do it). That might be in a diary entry, a photo you keep on file or share on social media or that is saved in your feel-good folder. You may want to let friends and family know so they can celebrate with you, or just keep it to yourself.

Chapter 2, pp. 43–50

If you found this challenging it may be because the only things that you see valued within academia are big wins that are tied to large-scale ventures and equivalent funding. You can include anything you like here – it can be within or outside academia and works better if you aren't just marking 'official' successes as measured by someone else. You can note as you do this how often we don't give ourselves credit if it's not approved by others.

Reflect and remember

When life is busy or stressful it's easy to lose track of the good things going on. You can either plan for great stuff or remember wonderful moments with:

#HappinessJournals – where you log positive thoughts, plan special treats, or note memorable moments and things you are proud of. Some happiness journals are part-completed for you to fill in (see *Set your own schedule* above).

Stickers – these can be combined with either happiness journals or scrapbooking, using bespoke stickers with positive messages and images to annotate your stories.

#Scrapbooking – filled with holiday memories, documenting a relationship, representing family or friendship memories or recording your successes. Make your own or get ideas from hobby/craft shops.

#MemoryJars – at the start of the year get a clean jam jar and every time something good happens, write it on a scrap of paper and pop it in. At the end of the year spread out all the notes and see what made you happy through the last 365 days.

Interviewing yourself – answering questions to give you greater insights. You could write questions for a friend to answer, then swap. Or try Empowering Questions cards: https://sunnypresent.com/eq.

I keep lists of self-care tools and resources, which you may want to use or add to:

Suggestions for Self-Care
www.theresearchcompanion.com/selfcare_suggestions
Uplifting and inspiring ideas for you to try
www.theresearchcompanion.com/uplifting

Energise! www.theresearchcompanion.com/energise

The big list of calm www.theresearchcompanion.com/calm

These are a small selection of ideas. You'll find hundreds more online. You can also join community activities or swap self-care tips with friends. Remember in Chapter 2 the importance of caring for yourself as a radical act? However you decide to do it, don't stop!

References

Ahmed, S., 2017. *Living a Feminist Life*. Durham, NC: Duke University Press.

Cunha, L.F., Pellanda, L.C., Reppold, C.T., 2019. Positive Psychology and Gratitude Interventions: A Randomized Clinical Trial. *Frontiers in Psychology* 10, 584.

Hammond, P., 2018. CLANGERS for All, Every Day. Dr Phil Hammond. URL.

Kleon, A., 2019. *Keep Going: 10 Ways to Stay Creative in Good Times and Bad*. Workman PublishingNew York.

Lorde, A., 2018. *The Master's Tools Will Never Dismantle the Master's House*. London: Penguin Modern.

New Economics Foundation, 2008. *Five Ways to Mental Wellbeing*. London.

Pietrowsky, R., Mikutta, J., 2012. Effects of Positive Psychology Interventions in Depressive patients – A Randomized Control Study. *Psychology* 3, 1067–1073.

Seligman, M.E.P., Steen, T.A., Park, N., Peterson, C., 2005. Positive Psychology Progress: Empirical Validation of Interventions. *American Psychologist* 60, 410–421.

Sheldon, K.M., Lyubomirsky, S., 2006. How to Increase and Sustain Positive Emotion: The Effects of Expressing Gratitude and Visualizing Best Possible Selves. *The Journal of Positive Psychology* 1, 73–82.

8 Letting go, moving forward

'Moving on' – sounds a bit dramatic and flouncy. Endings can be satisfying – finishing off a paper you enjoyed or ending a successful module; going to a new job; defending your thesis; graduating; or ending a period of unemployment.

Alternatively your letting go might involve dropping things that aren't working for you anymore. So you might be:

- Saying 'no' to more tasks because your time is already full.
Chapter 7
- Looking for a new job, especially if your existing one leaves you feeling stressed, unhappy or unfulfilled; or if new qualifications entitle you to a more experienced/ senior role.
Chapter 5
- Switching career pathways if the one you've been following isn't giving you what you want or if you have been made redundant (see the end of this chapter for more resources).
- Giving notice on projects or events you're involved in if you feel unappreciated, your needs are not being met or you are being exploited.
Chapter 4
- Ending friendships or leaving groups or networks (on or offline) if they are making you feel miserable or

Chapter 2

exhausted, or are failing to make themselves more accessible and less prejudiced.

Chapters 5 and 6

- Moving away from a place or person that is causing you mental, physical, sexual or financial harm.
- Admitting/accepting when a project or paper isn't working and looking to leave it for a while, delegate it or abandon it.

Chapters 1, 3 and 5

Many messages within academia are based around resilience, persistence and tenacity. In such an environment letting go can feel counterintuitive; forcing us to remain in situations that may be harmful or destructive. Moving on may feel fantastic as soon as you decide to make that change. Or you may need to plan and prepare before actions become a reality. If you're being bullied at work you might not be able to leave immediately because you need an income and have to work on your confidence, but you could start looking for other jobs right now; and if you're really being made unwell by academia see your doctor (if available) and get signed off work. Alternatively

Chapters 2, 4 and 6

you might want a complete career break but need to retrain, in which case you can plan that as a longer-term goal.

Chapter 1

We can hang onto work, people or activities because it's our anchor, identity or safety net. Despite being chronically unwell and struggling financially during my PhD I wouldn't quit my studies, believing without them I'd have nothing left. This definitely motivated me – and harmed my mental and physical health. Perhaps giving up might have been a better choice? Equally when I was made redundant a few years ago I felt my identity had been ripped away and it took me some time to acknowledge that while I had to leave some things behind, I could appreciate how much I could carry forward. Sometimes with all the reflections and preparations life will just happen and it's better to go with what you have than berating yourself for not making different choices.

Planning changes, big or small, may be more effective and reassuring if you work with people you trust. Talking over your options, working together to support each other, and noting whether the things you are holding onto are helping or holding you back. You might want to record conversations about what you want to leave/quit and how you might achieve that. Or sketch out an escape plan. Or draw, collage or scrapbook what you are going to let go and where that will take you. Making changes can be emotional, so whatever it is you are reflecting on it's best to build in self-care and rest.

Leaving academia

You never have to leave academia, unless you want to. If you're currently unhappy this may be your plan. Or it might be that there are other vocations or courses of study that appeal. Often 'leaving academia' is wrongly interpreted as 'leaving university' because the myth you can only be an academic in a university is so pervasive. As mentioned right at the start, academia covers a vast range of jobs and study opportunities, so 'leaving' might mean:

Switching departments – for example moving from Sociology into Health and Social Care; or swapping cleaning college residences to servicing conference facilities.

Switching disciplines/trades – swapping being a porter to working in the post room; or changing from mathematics to economics.

Retraining to undertake an entirely different role or for a more senior position.

Staying in the same work/subject area but *moving to a different academic institution*.

Changing the degree/subject you are studying, either within your current university or by switching to another college.

Continuing with the job you had in a university, but *using those skills elsewhere* – for example moving from a mathematics department to working for a polling company; leaving anthropology to work for a humanitarian organisation; or shifting work as a security guard in a university to a hospital.

Becoming self-employed – using the skills you acquired in one place (e.g. IT, project management, writing skills) to support individuals or organisations with their teaching, research or other needs. [Note: lots of people are currently leaving universities and deciding to set themselves up as consultants with a plan to advise colleges on better practice. This is a highly competitive market and worth remembering – if they didn't listen to you or pay you fairly while in a post what makes you think this will have changed? Don't assume the only places that want or need your skills are universities, there are plenty of other businesses, organisations and charities to try!].

Doing something else entirely – your skills are transferable. You may be more fulfilled, happier or less stressed in a completely different place. You may find on calculating your pay versus how much you work that you might earn the same or more in a different job with better working conditions.

Only you can decide, but don't keep pushing yourself to stay in a place that does not respect you, support you,

Chapter 4

encourage you or make you feel wanted and welcome. Life is too short.

Make a skills inventory

You may be unsure about your current role or feel you deserve a change but may not know what to include, especially if things have been difficult or your confidence is low. If you've been working or studying in academia you'll have numerous skills and abilities that you may not be showcasing, some of which may be outlined in the table below and others you may recognise are missing that you can add.

Skill/ability/ experience	What you can do
Tech	Using different computer packages, software, programming and devices for work and study.
Writing	Applying different writing techniques to describe ideas; make arguments; create reports; document events or activities; take notes; and make complex ideas more easily understood.
Presenting	Being able to share ideas, information and arguments across different formats including oral presentations; posters; websites; vlogs; podcasts; talks; workshops; or on social media. If you speak different languages (including signing) these are relevant here.

(continued)

Skill/ability/ experience	What you can do
Funding	Manage finances, create budgets, bid for funding, deliver on paid-for projects.
Impact and sustainability	Create events, activities or projects that deliver measurable and sustainable outcomes.
Library/search skills	Being able to find and read different publication formats (books, papers, reports, monographs) and synthesise complex information into clear messages and arguments.
Research	Use a variety of different methodologies (aka research skills) to identify problems/questions and find answers/explore ideas, analyse data, then draw conclusions and make recommendations.
Leadership	Enabling other people to work or study; supporting them to progress; identifying any training needs they may have; providing pastoral care, mentoring or supervision. Plus hosting and chairing meetings, dealing with feedback, teaching and collaborating.
Teamwork	Working with other people to identify and solve problems, complete tasks, share ideas and empower and support one another.

Project management	Run a project from idea to dissemination; identify possible problems or barriers; work with different communities/stakeholders; be realistic about tasks and timelines; work in flexible and responsive ways.
Self-directed working	The ability to plan; manage time, workload and tasks; stick to deadlines; make strategic changes as needed. Being able to work in an accurate, responsible and trustworthy way without requiring close supervision.
Problem solving and critical thinking	Identifying problems, causes and solutions. Processing and synthesising information from a variety of different sources. Testing questions and ideas.
Inclusive practices	Being aware of who is left out and why, and how they may be made welcome, including an awareness of rights and accessibility issues and accommodations.

Chapter 4

You may find working with a friend helps you identify key skills each of you has forgotten or overlooked. Searching online for key words like 'skills inventory' or 'transferable skills' can also identify things you can do that may be an ideal fit for a job or volunteering position you've not previously considered. Or show you where, with some additional training or study, you might be able to achieve more. Once you think about yourself in this way you may feel a lot stronger, more confident and aware of just how much you've already achieved and could offer.

If you found this challenging it may be because it's a daunting task or you initially believe there is little you have to offer. If you plan time to work on your skills list, rather than trying to do it in one go, and break down every single thing you can do to identify all the actions and abilities required to make it happen it may be clearer. Remember, this isn't a competition, it's an invitation to recognise you are able to do way more than you probably appreciate and that outside of work-/study-based tasks there will be many more positive personal attributes you possess.

Find out more

Beyond the Professariate (career advice by and for PhDs):
https://beyondprof.com
From PhD to Life (offers information on academic careers that don't just include universities):
https://fromphdtolife.com
Preparing for Academic Practice
www.apprise.ox.ac.uk/academic_career_paths
The Leveraged PhD https://theleveragedphd.com
Social Research Association http://the-sra.org.uk
National Coalition of Independent Scholars www.ncis.org
If you're seeking another job try individual university or organisational websites; plus look for 'Find a Job', 'Higher Education' and 'Funding' on this link:
https://theresearchcompanion.com/resources
Roostervane: Career Direction for Lost Academics
https://roostervane.com
The Para Academic Handbook
www.hammeronpress.net/shop/precarity/the-para-academic-handbook

At the end of the day/before finishing work

1 Think back over your day. Ask yourself 'how did it go? How do I feel? What were the best parts?'

Chapter 7, pp. 218–219

2 Do you need assistance? Or need to report something that's gone wrong? Speak to your supervisor and use your support network.

Chapter 4

Chapter 2

3 Check in with anyone you're responsible for/care about (your students, colleagues, family etc).

Chapters 3 and 4

4 Was there anything hard or difficult about today? Recognise you did the best that you could.

Chapter 7

5 Let any worries go (for now). They might have resolved themselves by tomorrow and, if they haven't, you'll be able to deal with them then, using any support you need or entitlements you deserve.

Chapter 7

Chapters 2 and 4

6 Focus on enjoying the time you have free to care for your wellbeing; rest, relax, revive or do whatever it is that brings you pleasure.

Chapter 6

Chapter 7

I hope you've found this book useful. And that if you felt alone when you began it, you now feel supported. It may be there are things you still want to talk about or issues you want to explore. Keep doing that with your networks and I'll continue the conversation with free resources and advice at www.theresearchcompanion.com and on social media. I'm @drpetra on Twitter, and @petraboynton on Instagram where I share daily tips and materials. Make sure to use the hashtags #BeingWellInAcademia and the #ResearchCompanion so we can all find each other and swap resources and advice.

Chapter 2

Find out more

The following books may be useful if you want to take forward some of the ideas shared here in your organisation.

Higher Education, Pedagogy and Social Justice: Politics and Practice. Kelly Freebody, Susan Goodwin and Helen Proctor (eds) (2019), Palgrave Macmillan.

Re-imagining Curriculum: Spaces for Disruption. Lynn Quinn (2019), African Sun Media.

Generous Thinking: A Radical Approach to Saving the University. Kathleen Fitzpatrick (2019), John Hopkins University Press.

Wellbeing in Doctoral Education: Insights and Guidance From the Student Experience. Lynette Pretorius, Luke Macaulay and Basil Cahusac de Caux (eds) (2019), Springer.

Identity and Pedagogy in Higher Education: International Comparisons. Kalwant Bhopal and Patrick Alan Danaher (2010), Bloomsbury.

Indigenous Pathways, Transitions and Participation in Higher Education: From Policy to Practice. Jack Frawley, Steve Larkin and James A. Smith (eds) (2017), Springer.

Thanks for reading *Being Well in Academia*! Remember, stick together and never be afraid to reach out for help.
   I wish you well.

Index